MOVING
BEYOND
G·R·I·E·F

Discovery House PUBLISHERS

BOX 3566 · GRAND RAPIDS, MI 49501

*PUBLISHING BOOKS THAT FEED
THE SOUL WITH THE WORD OF GOD.*

MOVING BEYOND G·R·I·E·F

Lessons From Those Who Have Lived Through Sorrow

RUTH SISSOM

Dedicated to the One
Who comforts us in all our trials

Moving Beyond Grief
Copyright © 1994 by Ruth M. Sissom

Library of Congress Cataloging-in-Publication Data

Sissom, Ruth M., 1932–
    Moving beyond grief : lessons from those who have lived through sorrow / Ruth M. Sissom.
    p.   cm.
    ISBN 0-9929239-09-1
    1. Bereavement—Religious aspects—Christianity. 2. Consolation.
    3. Death—Religious aspects—Christianity. I. Title.
    BV4905.2.S575   1994
    248.8'6—dc20   94-15196
                                                  CIP

Discovery House Publishers is affiliated with Radio Bible Class, Grand Rapids, Michigan 49512

Discovery House books are distributed to the trade by Thomas Nelson Publishers, Nashville, Tennessee 37214

Printed in the United States of America

94 95 96 97 98 99 / CHG / 10 9 8 7 6 5 4 3 2 1

Text Credits

P. 64—**Peace in the Midst of the Storm**, copyright © 1977, Pilot Point Music/ASCAP, all rights reserved, administered by ICG, Inc., used by permission; p. 73—**Footprints**, used by permission of Margaret Fishback Powers; p. 139—**He Is Able**, copyright © 1988 Maranatha! Music, administered by The Copyright Company, used by permission.

Every effort has been made to establish sources and obtain permission for the lyrics and poetry used in this book. If readers have any information leading to the positive identification of authors of any original work, please contact the publisher at the address given in the back of this book.

CONTENTS

ACKNOWLEDGMENTS

With deep appreciation I acknowledge the courageous people who shared glimpses into the intimacies of their hearts for the purpose of helping others through this book.

Special thanks to my brother, Dr. John Landon, who had more faith in my ability to write than I had in myself.

Sincere appreciation to the following for the sacrifice of self in order that this message of hope and courage could become a reality:

My daughter, Carol, for patiently proofreading and formatting my manuscript, and for teaching me the wonders of the computer.

My friend Evelyn, for many hours spent in proofreading.

My son, Paul, and my son-in-law, Glenn, for helping me solve the computer puzzle.

And to Carol Holquist, Associate Publisher, Discovery House, for graciously answering my many questions and encouraging me.

1

Introduction:
Through the Valley
of the Shadow

"I am so angry at God!" The woman who spoke these words was attractive and fashionably dressed, yet the stylishness of her ensemble was completely canceled out by the cold rage that seemed to emanate from her. She had come up to me at the conclusion of my presentation at a conference on Responding to Loss. The moment I saw her, I was struck by the tautness of her face, the set of her jaw, her clenched teeth and clenched hands, and the icy glare in her eyes. Her body was rigid with fury. Even the fur of her lovely mink coat and hat seemed to bristle!

I put my arm around her shoulders, silently praying that God would help me find the words to give her some measure of comfort. "It's all right to feel angry," I said.

"I'm so disappointed with God!" she continued. "He took my husband sixteen months ago. I did everything I could think of that God might want me to do. Why did He take my husband away? Why?"

I hugged her closer, but her body remained as unyielding as the anger within her. I studied the pain that was etched in her face—and I recognized that pain. My heart ached for another widow struggling with the awful hurt of a deep loss.

Tears welled up in the woman's eyes and spilled down her cheeks, evidence not only of her anger but of the deep sorrow within her. "I can't talk to God anymore," she said. "I can't go to church. I can't read the Bible. I'm just . . . so . . . angry!"

We talked for a few minutes, and I tried to offer hope and a few practical suggestions that could help her work through the grief and anger she was feeling. She didn't see any point in trying my suggestions. I desperately wished there was some way to reach her, some way to give her just a glimpse of healing, a glimmer of God's love. As we talked, she made just one statement that gave me a ray of hope. "My friends told me to come to this conference," she told me, "but it just makes me feel worse." She had friends! There were people who cared about her, who listened to her, who wanted to help her—and she was talking with them! I knew that one of the keys to emotional healing is being able to express feelings.

With my arm still around her, I said, "I know this is hard for you to accept right now, but God really does understand how angry you feel toward Him. He loves you and accepts your feelings. He wants you to tell Him how you feel, just as honestly as you have been telling me. Please don't give up talking to God—and be sure to continue talking with your friends. I'd also encourage you to work through these feelings with a pastor or counselor. Believe me, I know. It will get better with God's help."

She showed little response to what I said. I don't know if my words reached her or not, because she turned at that moment and disappeared into the crowd of people who had gathered around to talk with me after my presentation. I regretted not asking for her phone number. I wish I could have talked to her later, to see if she was making progress with her grief and anger.

In the months following that encounter, I've thought about this woman often, and I've prayed for her. She represents many people I've met whose emotional wounds continue to be raw and painful after months or years of grieving. Some become "stuck" in their pain. Their anger—which is normally a temporary stage in the grieving process—seems to settle into bitterness. I think of a young man who confided to me that his mother had become "a bitter old lady," and that none of her children enjoyed being around her since their father died. I think of a woman who spoke of her mother's twenty years of anger, and of her withdrawal into isolation following the death of her husband, a pastor.

I, too, have known the devastating pain and emotional confusion following the unexpected death of my husband. I wrote a book about the lessons God taught me as I traveled the arduous road to recovery. Following the publication of that book, **Instantly A Widow** (Discovery House, 1990), I received many opportunities to speak and proclaim God's grace and faithfulness to me. My purpose is to bring hope to those who suffer from loss and to stimulate greater sensitivity and understanding within those who care for the grieving. I have spoken to pastors, women's groups, church congregations, college students, and conference participants, and each time I speak, people share their experiences of loss with me. Some are coping well, but many are not. I want to do more to help inspire grieving people to continue moving on toward recovery and a truly satisfying life.

While pondering practical ways to challenge and encourage these people, my pastor asked me to develop a program of classes to help people who had lost loved ones. Drawing from my own personal knowledge of widowhood and my training and experience as a registered nurse, I put together a series of classes. Through these classes I became acquainted with many wonderful folks who were persevering on the road to recovery. One inspiring example is a woman named Reta.

"HE IS MY COMPANION NOW."

One month before his scheduled retirement, Reta's husband was diagnosed with cancer. Less than five months later, Reta was a widow. During their thirty-five years of marriage, Reta and her husband had done everything together. They were best friends. The sudden loss of her husband's companionship left Reta feeling desolate and disoriented.

One month after her husband's death, Reta joined a class I was teaching on recovery from loss. My heart went out to this lonely woman who seemed so frightened by her loss that she actually trembled. In the warm enclosure of our group, she found love and support from others who had lost loved ones—and she began to gain healing insights into her emotional needs. She later told me that a powerful discovery she made was that one of the best ways to heal our own hurts is to help others who are hurting. I saw her begin to reach out from the depths of her own pain to soothe the pain of other widows. She would take a grieving friend out to dinner or for a walk through the mall. Every time I arrived to lead other classes, I'd be greeted by Reta, and she would always bring a widowed friend or two—and sometimes even six or seven!

"I always try to maintain a happy spirit," she once told me. "I try to encourage people that God will see them through, just like He's doing for me. I tell them, 'Even though your heart is breaking, keep pressing on.'" The words of the Twenty-Third Psalm have become especially precious to Reta:

> The LORD is my shepherd,
> > I shall not be in want.
> He makes me lie down in green pastures,
> > he leads me beside quiet waters,
> > he restores my soul.
> He guides me in paths of righteousness
> > for his name's sake.
> Even though I walk
> > through the valley of the shadow of death,
> I will fear no evil,
> > for you are with me;
> your rod and your staff,
> > they comfort me.
> You prepare a table before me
> > in the presence of my enemies.
> You anoint my head with oil;
> > my cup overflows.
> Surely goodness and love will follow me
> > all the days of my life,
> and I will dwell
> > in the house of the LORD forever.

"That psalm," she says, "helps me realize that whatever I face in life, God is with me. He is my companion now in place of my husband."

NOT JUST SURVIVAL, BUT JOY

Reta is just one of many people who have been inspirational to me. As I thought about the examples of their lives, I began to think how they could serve as encouraging role models to others. I asked some of them if they would be willing to share their experiences. To my delight, they agreed.

In the following pages are the real-life stories of some of those courageous people. These are people who have felt the sting of death and the long, slow agony of grief as they have lost loved ones to such varied causes as Alzheimer's disease, heart attack, stroke, cancer, suicide, murder, a plane crash, and AIDS. These people speak with authenticity and simplicity. They know about the overwhelming feelings of anger, loneliness, guilt, and depression that come with a major loss. Some have persevered under emotional burdens so heavy it is nothing less than a miracle that they didn't give up.

All of these people recognized they had a choice to make: They could refuse God's comfort, drown in self-pity, withdraw into isolation, and sink into an ocean of life-long anger and bitterness. Or they could swim for dear life against the flood of their painful emotions, braving the rapids of life's most hostile circumstances, treading water across the deep, murky sea of despair, clinging to God until they came into the safe harbor of His healing. Sink or swim? These people chose to swim.

Those of us who are facing grief, or who love someone who is facing grief, have many questions to ask these people:

"What was the biggest problem you had to overcome?"

"What kinds of things did people do for you that really helped you?"

"What did people do that you wished they hadn't done?"

"How have you been able to recover your hope and your optimism after such a shattering loss?"

"How did your faith in God survive?"

"Will the pain ever end? And if so, what do I need to do to get through it?"

In these pages you will journey with them, you'll weep with them, and you'll draw strength from their courage as you watch them cling to God through the descent into the valley of the shadow of death—and through the long climb back into the sunlight. You'll experience healing for your own broken heart as they share their insights, their stories, their poems, and their most comforting passages of Scripture. You'll learn not only how to survive your tragedy, but how to actually experience joy once again—the peace of God that passes understanding.

First, I want to introduce you to Becky, a woman who was all but destroyed by a loss few of us can imagine—the loss not only of her husband but of her three precious children. Turn the page, and Becky will tell her story in her own words . . .

"I was pregnant nine times," says Becky. "Three pregnancies ended in miscarriage. Three of our children died at a young age. And I thank God that three of our children are with me today. God gave me strength to endure the loss of those three precious children. Then He gave me the strength to care for my dying husband while I had cancer.

"It certainly wasn't because of anything I did that I survived all the suffering. I had no strength at all. God was my strength."

2
Becky's Story:
IT IS WELL WITH MY SOUL

When peace like a river attendeth my way
When sorrows like seabillows roll,
Whatever my lot, Thou hast taught me to say,
It is well, it is well with my soul.

Horatio B. Spafford

"Oh, Lord," I prayed, "if you want to take our precious little daughter, we are willing to give her up."

I was kneeling by the green overstuffed chair in the tiny apartment where we spent the first six years of our marriage, preparing for the ministry. During our first year, God gave us a beautiful baby girl, Diane Lou. At eleven months of age, she was diagnosed with progressive ulcerative colitis. For six months the doctors tried to treat her, but she continued to be in constant pain. Finally in a desperate effort to help her the doctor operated and tried a colostomy. I thought that would be the answer to her problem and she would be well. In spite of our hopes and prayers, Diane's condition only worsened. Following surgery, her condition was listed as critical, with little hope of recovery. My heart broke at the thought of losing her, yet it was also heartbreaking to see her suffer.

Finally I realized I had to release her to God to either heal her or take her. Only He knew what was best. As I prayed, a wonderful peace came over me. Just then the phone rang. It was the nurse at the hospital. "Come at once," she said. "Your daughter is dying."

"WAIT, MY DAUGHTER . . . "

My husband, Larry, and I rushed to the hospital. We were at her side as she took her last breath. I looked down at the little girl who had only been with us fifteen months, yet who had won such a big place in our hearts. She looked so peaceful. "The Lord giveth," I said, "and the Lord taketh away." I wasn't even aware I said those words, I was in such shock.

But some time later, the nurse who was with us at our daughter's bedside wrote me a letter. She said, "I was ready to give up my faith in God, but when I heard you quote that passage from Job, I turned my life completely over to Christ. I have prepared to go to the mission field." Because of the impact of our daughter's death, this nurse became a missionary nurse.

"The Lord giveth, and the Lord taketh away." I was pregnant when Diane died, so we experienced His giving at the same time we experienced the taking away. Our first son was born six months after Diane died. We named him Larry, after my husband. Our son was a healthy baby, and he developed normally. When he was three, our daughter Susan was born. She had health problems right from the beginning, including allergies and bronchitis. She came down with meningitis, complicated by pneumonia, when she was one year old. When she went into a coma, the doctors diagnosed encephalitis. I remember praying during my devotions that the Lord would intervene for Susan. God brought these words from Ruth 3:18 to my mind: "Wait, my daughter, until you find out what happens." And that is what I did.

For an entire year I visited Susan every day. She remained in a coma and I waited on the Lord. The doctors did everything possible, but her condition didn't improve. Again I came to a place where I had to go to my knees and pray, "I release her to you, Lord, You can take her." Again, as I did when I surrendered Diane to the Lord, I felt a strong sense of peace, an assurance that God was in control and would somehow bring His good out of our family's sorrow. It was as if a heavy burden was lifted from my shoulders.

The Lord took Susan home when she was two years old. Again, as when Diane died, we experienced God's giving and taking at the same time: I was pregnant again.

"WHERE IS GOD?"

When the baby was born, we named him Pauley, and we were glad that he, like his brother Larry, was a strong and healthy child. When Pauley was three years old, my husband accepted a call to a new church. This was a difficult time in our lives. It was the first time I had lived away from my family and friends, and I was very lonely. We had no established network of Christian friendships to support us. To add to our woes, there were major problems in the church. There had been two splits in recent years, and the congregation was divided into angry factions. On one occasion, Larry went to visit a lady in the church, and he introduced himself as the new pastor. "You," she replied acidly, "are not my pastor!" The situation in the church was stressful and disheartening—but the worst was still to come.

We had been at the church for about three months when three-year-old Pauley became sick. The glands in his neck were swollen, and the doctor believed it to be a mild case of mumps. Soon, however, his condition worsened and the doctor ordered him hospitalized. We stayed by Pauley's hospital bedside night and day. It was stressful and tiring for us all, yet Pauley took the entire ordeal with an amazingly cheerful, lovable, and compliant attitude. Even when the doctor had to perform a tracheotomy, Pauley cooperated willingly and obeyed the doctor's directions. But nothing the doctors did seemed to help. Pauley's condition deteriorated until it was clear that there was no hope of recovery.

I recall walking around the hospital grounds with my husband, just to get some fresh air. We were both feeling very angry toward God. Our life together was so full of pain and stress, and our hearts just ached for little Pauley. This would be the third child we would lose, and we felt it was so unfair for God to take yet another precious child from us.

"I don't think I can believe God anymore," said Larry. In a sense, I was shocked that he would say such a thing. He was a minister, after all. And yet there was a part of me that wasn't surprised at all, that actually accepted what Larry said as being completely natural—because I felt the same way.

Out of all the pain we felt, we were asking, "Where is God?" But we had no one to share our questions with. How could we voice such questions to anyone else? Larry was the pastor, I was the pastor's wife. We couldn't afford to be "real." We had to be an example to the people in our congregation. I realize now how this sense of feeling isolated and alone with our deepest feelings and questions actually compounded our pain and our problems. All of us—even pastors and their wives—need to have a few friends with whom they can totally be themselves, doubts, hurts, questions and all, and still be loved and accepted.

A short time later, Pauley passed away, and we were again faced with making funeral arrangements for a little child. There is something so devastatingly sad about picking out a child's casket and the little clothes he will wear. But God comforted me by bringing to my mind the song, "Does Jesus Care?"

> Does Jesus care when I've tried and failed
> To resist some temptation strong;
> When for my deep grief I find no relief,
> Though my tears flow all the night long?
>
> Does Jesus care when I've said "good-bye"
> To the dearest on earth to me,
> And my sad heart aches
> Till it nearly breaks—
> Is it aught to Him? Does He care?
>
> O yes, He cares;
> I know He cares,
> His heart is touched with my grief;
> When the days are weary,
> The long nights dreary,
> I know my Savior cares.
>
> —Frank E. Graeff

These comforting words had been playing and replaying in my mind since Pauley's death. As we walked into the funeral home, the organist was playing this same song, and I felt God was reaching out to me in my grief.

Yet, even in the midst of our grief over Pauley, the swirling, wounding circumstances of our lives refused to let up. I was in the funeral home, consumed with sorrow, when one of the funeral directors called me to the phone. My doctor was calling with an urgent message about my remaining son, ten-year-old Larry. He had been sick, and the doctor had just received some test results back. "If you don't want your other son to die," the doctor said bluntly, "you must take him to the hospital in Ann Arbor as soon as possible. He has the same disease Pauley had."

I was shaking as I put down the phone. I can't handle any more, I thought. I'm drowning in my grief now! I can't give up another child!

A YEAR OF GRIEVING AND HEALING

We were caught in an emotional and spiritual bind. We knew we had to trust the Lord to take care of Larry, but after losing three of our four children, we wondered if trust was even possible. But we continued to pray and to hope, and eventually the Lord did heal Larry of the disease that took Pauley—a disease that was considered fatal at that time. It was a strange emotional mix, filled with contradictory feelings, after Larry came through his crisis. Though we continued to feel angry and disappointed with God because of Pauley's death, we were able to find it in our hearts to praise Him for healing Larry.

In the months that followed, we were emotionally and physically drained, but we put one foot in front of the other and kept moving forward with our lives and with our church work. We had to be quiet and wait for God to give us back our joy. It was more than a year before we could get beyond the anger and grief. But in time, the Lord restored our courage and strength.

During that year of grieving, I would often go to Pauley's upstairs bedroom, look out the window to the sky, and picture Pauley in heaven in Jesus' arms. That was one of the comforts God gave me. My thoughts would go back a few months when Pauley was laughing and playing. He saw the garbage truck coming down the street and he came running in the house proclaiming, "When I grow up I want to be a garbage man!"

God also gave me comfort through music, since it was such an important part of my life. He strengthened me through His Word. He would give me just the right verse for that particular day—verses such as Nahum 1:7, "The Lord is good, a stronghold in the day of trouble," and Deuteronomy 33:27, "The eternal God is your refuge and underneath are the everlasting arms." I remember ironing the clothes and I didn't have to sprinkle them because my tears dampened them. Sometimes my heart was so heavy I just called out to God to help me—and the Holy Spirit would come and speak peace to my heart.

MAKING SENSE OUT OF SENSELESSNESS

I was pregnant when Susan died and when Diane died. When Pauley passed away, we again experienced God's giving and taking at the same time: I was pregnant again, this time with another daughter. Anticipating her arrival, along with my church activities, helped to keep my mind off my sorrows. But throughout that period, the words of Job 1:27 kept coming back to my mind: "The Lord gave and the Lord has taken away; blessed be the name of the Lord."

I went to counsel at Lake Ann camp and while I was there I received a telegram that my sister had passed away. It was another blow to my already aching heart. I shared with the teenage girls in my cabin that God was my strength in grief, and every one of those girls made a decision for Christ. It was enormously uplifting for me to see some good come out of the tragedy I was going through.

Time went by, and with every week I received strength from the Lord. I kept busy teaching a Sunday school class, singing in the choir, and playing piano. Seven months after Pauley died, Barbara was born.

For much of that first year after Pauley's death, I wondered if any good could come from such a seemingly senseless tragedy as the death of a child. In time, however, we saw that healing could come even from this terrible sorrow. We began to see the Lord using Pauley's death to unify our troubled church. Perhaps it was the way this tragedy brought home to people the fact that life is short and we should spend it on the things that matter, not on petty squabbles and bickering among Christian brothers and sisters. Perhaps it was the fact that people from various factions were able to set aside their anger, and to unite in a broken heart for little Pauley, and in lovingly walking with us through our grief. In any case, we saw hurts being healed and bitterness purged from human hearts. The people were drawn closer to the Lord and to each other.

As the church grew in numbers and in a unified spirit, we launched a building program and constructed a lovely church facility with mostly volunteer help. The Lord sent competent workers at exactly the right time. When it was time for brick work to be done, a bricklayer "just happened" to be passing through our area and asked us if we needed help (he did an excellent job, too!). When it came time for electrical work, the Lord sent us an electrician. A man from our membership did the plumbing. The Lord blessed every phase of the project. The church grew and many came to know the Lord.

Two years after Barbara's birth, God gave us another daughter, Cindy. That was my ninth pregnancy. I had three miscarriages, we lost three of the children who were born to us, and I thank God that three of our children are alive and healthy today. God gave me strength to endure the loss of those three precious children. But I was going to need a lot more strength, because there were still more losses on my horizon.

Larry's x-ray

We moved to a new church and our work was going well. By this time Larry and Barbara were both married and in their own homes. Cindy was eighteen. My husband, Larry, and I had enjoyed 35 years of marriage, and throughout all that time his health had been very good. Then he developed a little cough.

When the cough wouldn't go away, Larry went to see a doctor. The doctor checked him, and found no reason for major concern. "But just to be sure there is no problem," he told Larry, "we'll take a chest x-ray." It was a Wednesday evening, as we were getting ready for prayer meeting, when the doctor phoned with the report. "The x-ray shows a large mass on Larry's lung," the doctor said. "I'm afraid he'll need surgery."

Choir practice followed prayer meeting. The song we practiced was, "I'll Praise Your Name Lord, and Sing Your Song." I thought, How can I ever sing this song? But, with trembling lips and a fearful heart, I sang the best I could.

Immediately after Larry's operation, the surgeon came to us and gave us the dreadful news. "It's cancer," he said. "I'm afraid the life expectancy is probably about seven months."

"How could this possibly be true?" was the question I kept asking myself. My husband was 56 years old and in the prime of his ministry. He was a church builder—an able, responsible, committed man of God. Why would God take him when he was so active for God and so needed by his church?

Larry's condition deteriorated rapidly and I cared for him during those seven months of his final illness. The first few months following the surgery were emotionally difficult for him and for me. He was uncomfortable, depressed, and irritable, and I found it difficult to share my truest feelings with him. It was clear, looking back, that we both needed some time to accept what was happening— that Larry really was approaching the end of his life.

In time, however, he did reach a place of acceptance, a place where he could say, in effect, "I realize there is no hope of recovery, and that's okay. I've trusted God with my life, and I'll just have to trust Him with my death as well." Once Larry reached that place of acceptance, the Lord seemed to give him peace. He even felt free to plan his entire funeral service. Toward the end, we became closer and shared together everything we were thinking and feeling.

I didn't feel well during those months as I cared for my husband. I was losing weight and I knew something was wrong, but my husband needed me. My health was secondary to his great need. I felt that crying showed weakness, so I kept the emotion inside a long time. I wanted to be strong for Larry. But when I finally began to cry, I sobbed and sobbed. It was as if, once the floodgates were open, I would never get them closed again. I believe that keeping my feelings bottled up inside me was a major reason I experienced a number of physical and emotional problems.

Larry's last public appearance was his participation in our son's ordination to the ministry. Larry was thin, uncomfortable, and quite ill, but he managed to preach the message. I remember that day as a day of emotional extremes. One moment I felt great pride and joy as I looked at our son entering the ministry for the Lord and following in his father's footsteps. The next moment I felt a wave of sadness wash over me as I knew I was about to lose my husband.

Larry's message was symbolic of an enormous loss that was rolling inexorably into our lives. It meant that our life together was ending. It meant Larry's ministry as a pastor was ending. It meant his physical life was ending. Larry was passing the torch to his son, but his race was over. It was all over! I can't describe the depths of the ache I felt as I pondered these losses.

About a month later, the Lord took Larry home to heaven.

At the funeral, I felt a lot of pressure to be a "perfect" example to our congregation—not pressure from the church, or from anyone else. It was pressure that came from within myself. I remember when my husband's casket was carried out of the church, a lot of eyes were on me, watching for my response, wondering how the pastor's wife would react. I felt they were looking at me, thinking, You're a Christian. Can you handle this? Though my heart was breaking, I made myself smile.

I believe how we handle adversity can be a great testimony of God's power to those looking on. But the pressure to be a "perfect" example to other people came from my own unrealistic expectations. Thanks to many gracious friends in the church, I now understand that you can also be a Christian example by being honest about your pain and your feelings. If I had it to do over again, I think I would just be myself.

GETTING THROUGH THE GRIEF . . . AGAIN

The grief process that followed Larry's death was long, deep, and devastating. I rewalked many of the same paths of despair I had experienced after Pauley's death. Sometimes I felt close to God and at other times He seemed very distant. I was so hurt that at times I could only fall down on my knees and say, "Help!" No other words would come. I'm grateful for the Holy Spirit who understands our groanings and intercedes for us. When I felt so alone I just sat and listened to tapes of pastors' messages. I prayed, "Lord, you know how I feel. You know me better than I know myself. You'll just have to take care of me. Even though You seem so distant I know You are here."

After Larry's death it dawned on me that my children were hurting just as much as I was. I had been so engrossed in caring for my husband I seemed to forget about my children's feelings. I remember Barbara telling me she cried so much at work she thought she would be fired. When we began sharing our grief, our family came together as a very close unit.

There were many resources and kindnesses that helped me through that time I spent in the valley of the shadow of death—a valley I had already spent so much time in during my life. Some of my favorites:

The wonderful books and cards from Christian friends. **Those Who Hurt,** by Charles Swindoll was an especially helpful book.

The notes people wrote on their cards.

The healing messages God gave me again and again from the Scriptures that helped me go on. I'd get up in the morning, open my Bible, and say, "Lord, give me something that will help me through this day," and He would lead me to just the right verse to give me strength. I leaned on I Corinthians 10:13, which says that God is faithful, and won't allow us to be tested beyond what we can bear, but will give us the strength we need to withstand it.

It took me a long time for me to adjust to life without my husband. I remember going to a great conference or meeting, and I'd think, I can't wait to get home and share this with Larry. Then suddenly I would realize, **Larry's gone!** It was lonely in the big empty parsonage all by myself. My loneliness drew me closer to the Lord and He has become my husband since I've been a widow. I can go to Him like I used to go to Larry with my problems.

"WHEN SORROWS LIKE SEABILLOWS ROLL . . . "

One month after Larry died I was diagnosed with cancer. I had neglected the tumor for so long while I cared for my dying husband that it was inoperable until it could be reduced by radiation treatments. The surgery was followed by a year of chemotherapy. There was little hope for my recovery.

All through that hard time, not knowing whether I would live or die, I talked to God as I would have talked to my husband. He gave me comfort through a song called "Finally Home." Larry and I had talked a lot about where we would finally settle and make our home. We had moved many times and always lived in parsonages. Even before he was diagnosed with cancer, we had concluded that our home would be heaven. Larry had arrived there first, and now he was waiting for me. All during my cancer treatments, I was reminded through that song that if God did not heal me I would finally be home with Larry.

Another hymn, "It is Well With My Soul," helped give me courage to commit my illness and future to God, knowing He was in control and would work everything out for the best. That hymn was written by a man who understood what I had been through, because he wrote it while his own heart was breaking, soon after his four daughters were lost at sea during a storm. He knew the deepest grief that "sorrows like seabillows" can bring, yet he was able to say, "it is well with my soul." So these words were an enormous comfort to my heart and a challenge to my spirit:

> When peace like a river attendeth my way
> When sorrows like seabillows roll,
> Whatever my lot, Thou hast taught me to say,
> It is well, it is well with my soul.

My husband used to tell people, "We need to walk closely with the Lord, because just one telephone call can change you life." We had received a number of those life-changing telephone calls over the years, and I deeply wanted to rely on God and trust Him. Life became a moment-by-moment proposition, and every one of those moments was precious.

God did heal me of the cancer. But I still had my life to live and a lot of adjustments to make after Larry died. His loss left a gaping hole in my life. I noticed the loss most in all the little everyday aspects of life. I remember the first time I had to balance the checkbook by myself, I sat down and cried. My husband handled all the finances until his illness, and then I gradually had to take charge of the money. Not only was that a struggle for me, but it also was an emotional symbol of the fact that Larry was really gone and I was on my own.

Another dilemma I faced was deciding where to live. When I had to leave the parsonage, my son and his wife, Sandy, invited me to live in their basement apartment for a year. The Lord worked everything out for me down to the smallest detail. He opened one door, then another; He resolved this difficulty, then eased me out of that one. It was really like having the Lord as my husband! He provided everything I needed.

Another difficult trial was the loss of my sister to cancer. My mother had died when I was nine, and my father had died when I was ten, so it was this sister who had raised me and been like a mother to me since I was very young (I was the youngest of eight children). More recently, she had been a missionary in Peru for twenty-five years. I cared for her in the hospital during the last five weeks of her life, as she struggled with terminal cancer. It was the least I could do after all she did for me when I was a child.

PREPARE FOR THE INEVITABLE

We don't like to admit it. We don't even like to think about it, but it's true: Death and grief are inevitable. I believe the wise thing, when faced with the inevitable, is to prepare ourselves for it. How do you prepare today for the grief that is sure to come tomorrow?

Read the Bible and have a daily walk with the Lord. As you saturate your mind in the truths of God's Word, you implant healing truths that God can bring back to your mind when you need them.

Remember that whatever the affliction, it has been appointed and approved by God our Heavenly Father for our good. Praise God for everything that comes into your life even though it is hard.

Find your source of comfort in God, through the Bible and through listening to the still, small voice of His Spirit.

Delay making any major decisions for the first year. Your thinking processes are not as acute during the emotionally confusing time of intense grieving. Many people make major mistakes during their grieving period, and deeply regret them months later when their perspective returns to normal.

Allow yourself to grieve without feeling ashamed or guilty. The emotions you bottle up are likely to come out in some other way—probably through a physical or emotional ailment. In my own case, I believe the emotions I repressed after the deaths of my three children brought about an emotional breakdown. I am still under a psychiatrist's care today. I attribute my cancer and emotional problems to my failure to appropriately grieve the many losses I had to deal with.

Exercise regularly. Physical exercise is essential during grief, even if no more than a walk around the block each day.

Eat nourishing food. This is important to rebuild our bodies and maintain health.

Reach out to others. God gave me opportunities to help people. My daughter, Cindy, who is a nurse, told me about a lady who had surgery and needed someone to stay with her. I had cared for my ill husband for seven months, so I knew how to help people in that situation. After that lady recovered, others began to ask if I could help them. I cooked, sat with folks, and helped them during their various illnesses. I soon discovered many people were worse off than I was and as I helped them, my grief was gradually healed.

Stay involved with your family. My daughter, Barbara, needed a sitter for her three boys. I offered to help her. I enjoy my grandchildren and the opportunity to be an influence in their lives.

CARING FOR THE GRIEVING

You would think that after all the funeral home and hospital experience I have gone through I would be an expert on how to help people who are grieving, but I still feel quite inadequate. If there is one important thing I've learned about caring for the grieving, it would be this: Just be there. Standing by the grieving one is usually all you need to do. Sometimes silence is the best way you can comfort another. Don't feel you have to say anything or quote a Bible verse. Just be there and show your love.

I feel that God is receiving all the glory for what has happened through my life. It certainly wasn't because of anything I did that I survived all the suffering. I think I must have been in shock a lot of the time because I don't even remember many things that happened. I had no strength at all. God had to be my strength—my all. He used my pain and sorrow in many ways, including sending that nurse as a missionary at Diane's death and unifying our church when Pauley died.

I still wonder at times why God took my husband instead of me. I was weak and had health problems. He was the strong one, the leader, the church builder. My children and I have found comfort in the first two verses of Isaiah 57:

> The righteous perish,
>   and no one ponders it in his heart;
> devout men are taken away,
>   and no one understands
> that the righteous are taken away
>   to be spared from evil.
> Those who walk uprightly
>   enter into peace,
>   they find rest as they lie in death.

It is comforting to realize that our loving Heavenly Father in His mercy and compassion spared my husband and our children from the many trials and evils they would have to face if they were still here. In this thought we are comforted and we put our trust in the Lord who does all things well, and we can say with the writer of the hymn, "It is well, it is well with my soul."

....

> On earth I'm a pilgrim and stranger,
> No place to abide for aye,
> But I have a home in God's heaven,
> I'm moving up home some day.

J. Vaughn

The God we learned to trust as small children sustained my sister, Marge, during the difficult years of her husband's illness and suicide, and through her recovery from loss. In this chapter, she shares some of her own poetry through which she found healing for her deep wounds of grief.

3

Marge's Story:
THE MEMORY BANK

"He gives strength to the weary
and increases the power of the weak.
Even youths grow tired and weary,
and young men stumble and fall;
but those who hope in the LORD
will renew their strength.
They will soar on wings like eagles;
they will run and not grow weary,
they will walk and not be faint."

Isaiah 40:20-31

I opened the door and the house was silent. "Honey, I'm home," I said, closing the door behind me. I was home from work, and expected to be greeted, as usual, by my husband, George. But he didn't answer.

"George," I called again, more loudly, "I'm home!"

Still no answer.

I felt a dreadful fear gripping me as I made my way downstairs to my husband's bedroom.

Then I saw him on the bed. In the waste basket were more than a dozen insulin syringes. He had taken an overdose. The big, strong, wonderful man I had married thirteen and a half years earlier was dead.

"REDUCE OR DIE."

I felt shock and terrible sadness. I also felt a sense of relief. For weeks, a heavy cloud of dread had been hovering over me, darkening my life. I was sure something like this was going to happen. So every day I lived in fear that this could be our last day together. Now it was over.

George's health had been deteriorating for several years. He refused to control his eating even though he was a diabetic on insulin. He was a compulsive overeater, a food-a-holic.

In a poem I wrote five years before his death, I expressed my fears over how extreme his problem had become. I never showed this poem to him.

DIE—ET?

He's always, always munching,
    On cookies, pop and cheeses,
His ice cream dish a cardboard box,
    To walk upstairs, he wheezes.

His legs cramp up at night, when he
    Has had too many sweets,
Feet and fingers tingle,
    Yet he eats—and eats—and eats!

And still he buys sweet groceries,
    A shopping trip a day.
Especially if they're bargains
    At stores along the way.

He's a real food-a-holic,
    Hides food in secret places,
Under a camping pillow
    Were two topping cases.

Hash in the clothes hamper,
    Spaghetti in the oven.
Geo's so busy eating
    He has no time for lovin'.

In his bathroom closet,
    I was surprised to see,
Two cases of large diet pop
    Staring out at me.

Blood pressure's at stroke level,
    Blood sugar's way too high,
Arthritis pains inflame his hip,
    Doctor says, "Reduce or die."

He only lives to eat, he says,
    He will not change his style,
Although he knows that down the road,
    This might be his last mile.

The diabetes affected his circulation and a large sore developed on his foot. Gangrene began appearing, and even though he knew he was running an extreme risk of amputation, he refused to submit to treatment. He just could not cope as his once-strong body steadily deteriorated. He became severely depressed. In desperation, I tried everything I could think of to help him. I had the doctor make house calls. I told his son, Frank, and daughter, Ruthie, about his desperate condition, hoping they could succeed where I had failed in convincing him to get treatment. Frank tried his best to reason with his dad and persuade him to get help, but George wouldn't budge.

George was a rugged individualist, determined to go his own way without any help from anybody. He would maintain control of his body, no one else, and he would control his circumstances, no matter what. Standing six feet, six inches tall and weighing 280 pounds, George had been a football player for Navy in his earlier days. He was one of the divers who helped raise the sunken **Normandy** and had taught diving at the Navy pier in New York City. He would rather be dead than submit to doctors, hospitals, and amputations.

As his body became sicker and weaker, his will became stronger. Through my tears, I pleaded with him, "George, you could live for many more years. Just listen to the doctor. Go to the hospital. Get treatment."

"No way!" he replied. "And don't bring it up again!" It was an ultimatum. I knew I was powerless to change his mind.

Then one evening, he wanted to talk. I can't believe I am doing this, I thought as I sat by George's bed with my yellow legal pad on my lap and my pen in hand.

"This is how I want things done," he said. "No funeral or other service of any kind. My body is to be given to science. If that cannot be done, I want to be cremated." He explained how he wanted the finances handled. It was like a bad dream. He dictated how things should be handled after his death and I took notes. He seemed so calm and matter-of-fact, but I was churning inside.

When the day I dreaded finally came, it began like any other day. I kissed him good-bye as I left for work in the morning. I came home at 5:30 p.m. and found him dead. Now it was up to me to carry out his wishes.

"Can't Cope, No Hope"

Expressing my thoughts and feelings through poetry is a great stress reducer for me. It's a way of purging pent-up emotions. Putting my feelings on paper and then reading and rereading them helped to heal the festering grief. Two months after George died, I reflected on what had happened and wrote the following poem.

CAN'T COPE ~ NO HOPE

It was quiet, deathly quiet,
    When I stepped inside the door,
I was home but George had left me,
    Left this world on February four.

Rough and rugged, tall and handsome,
    He was always in control,
Till poor health began to plague him,
    And it ate into his soul.

Less and less he walked and traveled,
    More and more he slept and read,
Said the effort wasn't worth it,
    Said he'd just as soon be dead!

Twice the doctor came and told him,
    "George, you have to be aware,
You will not get any better,
    If you sit here in this chair."

"Your foot has to get some treatment,
    And the hospital's the place,
Here, I can do nothing for you,
    You'll just leave the human race!"

George would listen so politely,
    But he still refused to go,
Hated hospitals, and doctors,
    Every time he answered, "No."

Frank and Judy came to visit,
    Flew from Memphis into snow,
Tried to change his mind, but couldn't,
    George said, "Absolutely no."

While ignoring doctor's orders,
    He got weak, (he'd been so strong),
It would mean an amputation,
    He had let it go too long.

When at last I knew he meant it,
    That he really planned to die,
I still hoped he'd never do it,
    I kept asking, "Why, oh why?"

Is there nothing left to live for?
    You could live for many years,
If you'd just obey the doctor,
    This, I told him, through my tears.

At the last, we talked of finance,
    Of cremation and of death,
If he couldn't will his body,
    What alternative was left?

George decided on cremation,
    With no service as his choice,
How could we make these decisions,
    In a normal tone of voice?

So I left that fateful morning,
    With a cheerful wave "good-bye."
Never dreaming for a moment,
    George would plan that day to die.

When I didn't get an answer
    To my call when I got home.
I just knew I had to face it,
    I must go downstairs alone.

As I came into the bedroom,
    George was peacefully in bed,
And I did not need a doctor,
    To tell me that George was dead!

Somehow, you spring into action,
    There are things that must be done,
Call the doctor, call the sheriff,
    Repeat facts to everyone.

With the medics and the sheriff,
    And the funeral director there,
I sat talking to the doctor
    From my insurance office chair.

We could not will George's body,
    As he long had specified,
Doctor ordered an autopsy,
    Had to find out how he died.

So I waited in the sunroom,
    While they took his body out,
Doug and Katherine both were with me,
    I was numb, inside and out.

We began to call the family,
    That was very hard to do,
Breaking news of death is awful,
    When it happens to be you.

Ruthie called—she'd planned to visit,
    Sad news made her call not long.
She would come on the same weekend,
    But her father would be gone.

Cards of sympathy and flowers
    Food and phone calls came that night,
We would honor George in some way,
    He would not drop out of sight.

So we set up a memorial,
    At the library down the street,
Where George was a regular patron,
    He was in there twice a week.

Life goes on and I am learning,
   To think "one" instead of "two,"
And I think of all the good times,
   And the things we used to do.

Of the trips and the adventures,
   When we put our rocks in sacks,
In the mines and in the mountains,
   Where we almost broke our backs.

Every rock within our garden,
   Really was a special stone,
We remembered where we'd found it,
   And the work to get it home.

George is gone, but not forgotten,
   And we mourn the way he died,
Painful days he couldn't cope with,
   So his choice was suicide.

There just has to be a lesson,
   We can learn because we care,
Faith in God could have prevented,
   George's feeling of despair!

Even through the copious tears of sadness I shed, I also experienced some relief. That shadowy cloud of doom that had hung over our life together had been lifted. The thing I feared had finally happened. At least now I could see more clearly exactly what I had to face.

I kept pondering what to do with George's ashes. I talked to his best friend, Jack. We agreed that George's favorite spot was a beautiful camping site on the Pine River. He loved the sound of wind rustling through the leaves of the trees that shaded the river. There George often sat to read and to watch canoeists floating by. He and Jack had spent many happy days in that area, camping, fishing, and cooking over an open fire. So we took George's ashes back to the Pine River Camp and buried them beneath his favorite tree.

BACK TO THE PINE

George is back at the Pine River,
   Where he loved to camp and fish,
Jack and I just took him back there,
   We knew that would be his wish.

It was on a sunny Friday,
    Jackson came for me at ten,
We drove off in his new pickup,
    That was how the trip began.

We turned onto the logging road,
    And wound our way along,
Through washouts and tight places,
    We heard a bluejay's song.

We came at last to the high bank,
    We stopped—and we stood still—
The steps that George and Jack had made,
    Would take us down the hill.

So we descended to the camp,
    So shaded by the trees
We stood upon the river's bank,
    Beneath the rustling leaves.

We sat in silence for awhile,
    And watched the river flow,
Where George had sat to read and cook
    And watch canoeists go.

Then—it was time, Jack dug a grave,
    We laid the box in gently,
And rolled a stone to mark the spot,
    And looked at it intently.

And then the tears began to come,
    I could not hold them back,
We could all three be standing here,
    Not just myself and Jack.

I wept for all the memories,
    Of times so long ago,
The camp, the beauty, and the food,
    And George who loved it so.

So—it was done—we climbed the steps,
    And got into the truck,
Driving up the washed out trail,
    We almost did get stuck.

We drove in silence for awhile,
    Each with our thoughts, alone,
And it was 7:30,
    When Jack left me at home.

This is the final chapter,
    George lies beneath the sod,
His grave is known to Jack and me,
    To wild things and to God.

RESOURCES FOR GRIEF

Burying George's ashes was the saddest time for me, but it also helped bring closure to the devastating events of the past four and a half months. I began to focus on my future and how I would cope with singleness. I had always had children or a husband with me. It was hard to imagine doing everything alone, and having no one with whom to share joys, sadness, plans, and dreams.

I had always been an independent person. I had worked full-time outside my home as well as operating a small insurance business from my home. I was used to taking care of household finances and making business decisions. These things were not a problem for me.

But guilt was!

I felt I should have prevented George's suicide. I told myself it was my fault. Finally I discussed my concerns with George's physician, and he was able to alleviate my guilt. He explained that it is common for survivors to feel guilty after a loved one commits suicide. "Even if you had been home all the time," he said, "there was no way you could have prevented George from committing suicide. You did everything humanly possible. George had his mind made up. He was determined and there was no stopping him."

I relied on several resources to get me through the grief process after George died:

I found it helpful to keep busy with my job. It gave me structure, routine, purpose, and a sense of accomplishment in my life.

I needed to talk through my feelings, and I found my brother (who is a minister) to be a patient, nonjudgmental listener.

I learned how important it is to express emotions, not hold them in. Before George's death, I used to pride myself on not crying at funerals, weddings, and other emotional occasions. But after his death, I found my eyes would brim with tears at the slightest urging: sentimental songs, a special anniversary date, a picture of a city we had visited together, any little thing. Birthdays and anniversaries stir many memories. I'm better now, but I still cry easily—and I think it's been therapeutic for me to ventilate those feelings.

I believe that the pain of loss can make us better Christians. Looking back over my own experience, I can see areas of personal growth that have been directly inspired by my trial of loss:

I depend more on God than ever before.

I have a deeper desire to know His will and to obey it.

I reach out to others and witness about God's love more than ever before.

I study the Bible more seriously than ever before. I no longer read random passages of Scripture; I now read and study the Bible more intentionally and systematically. Isaiah 40:31 has been a special source of strength:

> But those who hope in the LORD
> will renew their strength.
> They will soar on wings like eagles;
> they will run and not grow weary,
> they will walk and not be faint.

I find new meaning and value in the old hymns. When I was a child, my mother would rock me and my brothers and sister as she sang the old hymn, "Trust and Obey." The longer I sing it, the more meaningful it becomes. What a great truth it contains:

> Trust and obey,
> for there's no other way,
> to be happy in Jesus,
> but to trust and obey.

DEALING WITH DEPRESSION

When a loved one dies, there are so many legal things to do. There is a seemingly endless stream of death certificates required in order to have one for each transaction. Each certificate becomes a painful reminder of the horrible experiences surrounding the death of your loved one. Then, when the details are all taken care of and you are home alone, your eyes rest on his chair, his place at the table, his clothes—and it takes a strong person not to become depressed.

One of the most difficult tasks for me was to take George's clothes to the church collection box. It was a physically demanding and emotionally draining task to sort through so many reminders of George and of the days and events we shared together (there were eighteen huge plastic trashbags full). I cried many times as I went through those belongings.

I really believe that one of the most effective "antidepressants" I found was helping others. It's really therapeutic to get your mind off your own problems and loneliness, and to think about other people for a while. Through the grief process, I've become more sensitive to the emotions of others and their unspoken needs. There's an amazing principle at work here: If we choose to put our grief to work, demonstrating empathy and giving comfort to other grieving people, the healing is multiplied. We ourselves are helped and pulled out of our sorrow, even while we are helping to ease the sorrow of others. Here are some insights I discovered that have helped me to be more effective in standing by other people in their grief:

Offer your quiet, supportive presence. Don't avoid a grieving person because you don't know what to say.

Show you care. People coping with loss need to know that we care about them, and we can demonstrate caring without saying a word. An arm around the shoulder, a hug, a squeeze of the hand can communicate so much more than any words.

Pray for the person and ask God for the words to say to them that will bring comfort.

Avoid saying things like, "You shouldn't feel sad. Your loved one is in heaven now, and you should be happy." People should be given permission to express their true feelings, not urged to repress and deny their sorrow. When Lazarus died, Jesus wept—and we should weep, too, when a loved one dies.

Another resource that has helped me to move forward through grief has been finding a cause to believe in. When we pour our energies into a cause that's bigger than ourselves, we guard against becoming introspective and preoccupied with ourselves and our own problems. One of the causes I've been involved in, and which has been very therapeutic for me, is a national organization that recognizes professional women for their business accomplishments and service to the community. Through that organization, I've met women from across the United States who have made their communities and their world a better place.

Soon I'll retire from my job, so I'm looking forward to volunteer work in my local church and at the local library. I also seek opportunities through my church denomination to become involved in a cause that improves the status of women throughout the world.

Another resource for getting past depression and getting through the grief process is to keep memories alive. Memories don't die; they live on! All the years of life and happiness that George and I shared together are rather like a bank where I can go, withdraw a fund of memories, and treasure them. And the memories I withdraw today will be back in the bank, ready for withdrawal, when I return for them another day.

I hope that you and your loved ones are making precious deposits in the memory bank, so that someday you'll be able to draw from that endless supply of memories—with interest!

....

AT THE PLACE OF THE SEA

Have you come to the Red Sea place in your life,
Where, in spite of all you can do,
There is no way out, there is no way back,
There is no other way, but through?

Then wait on the Lord, with a trust serene,
Till the night of your fear is gone;
He will send the winds, He will heap the floods,
When He says to your soul,
"Go on!"

And His hand shall lead you through, clear through,
Ere the watery walls roll down;
No wave can touch you, no foe can smite,
No mightiest sea can drown.
The tossing billows may rear their crests,
Their foam at your feet may break,
But over their bed you shall walk dry-shod
In the path that your Lord shall make.

In the morning watch, 'neath the lifted cloud,
You shall see but the Lord alone,
When He leads you forth from the place of the sea,
To a land that you have not known;
And your fears shall pass as your foes have passed,
You shall no more be afraid;
You shall sing His praise in a better place,
In a place that His hand hath made.

—Annie Johnson Flint

Alice never drove a car or wrote a check before she lost her husband of forty-three years.

See how God was her source of strength as she tackled the seemingly impossible.

4

Alice's Story: GOD'S MIRACLE FOR A TREMBLING HEART

Under His wings what a refuge in sorrow
How the heart yearningly turns to His rest
Often when earth has no balm for my healing,
There I find comfort and there I am blest.

Under His wings, under His wings,
Who from His love can sever?
Under His wings my soul shall abide,
Safely abide forever.

William O. Cushing

It was Christmas Eve. My husband, Lloyd, and I were spending a quiet holiday evening at home. I began reflecting on our happy life together. Suddenly my pleasant memories were interrupted by a twinge of sadness and I shared my thoughts with Lloyd.

"Just think how lonely it would be if God took one of us," I remarked.

"I can't even imagine life without you," Lloyd replied.

Christmas came and went, and I forgot about that momentary twinge of melancholy. Then, on New Year's Eve, Lloyd and I were spending another quiet evening together, and I again felt a wave of sadness engulfing me. "Someday," I said, "we will celebrate a New Year together for the last time."

"The older I get, the more I think about it," Lloyd replied.

One month later, Lloyd entered the hospital for tests. The day he was discharged he said to me, "Get on your coat, we need to go to the bank. We need to get you a credit card."

As we went, Lloyd began to explain how to get our income tax returns done. Bewildered, I said, "Lloyd, why do I need to know all these things? You always take care of these matters."

"I won't be able to from now on," Lloyd replied. "I am going to die."

I was stunned. I kept thinking it had to be a mistake. The tests had to be wrong. But in the coming days, I was to find out that there was no mistake. My life was about to change forever, and my loving husband's life was about to end.

REDISCOVERING INDEPENDENCE

Lloyd became very frightened about leaving me alone. I had never written a check, never paid a bill, and did not know how to drive. He even went with me and filled out the papers for me when I had to go to the doctor. We were always together. We had a few friends, but we were content with each other and didn't go many places.

Over the next few days, Lloyd actively encouraged me to learn to drive, to write checks, and become more independent. "I know you can do it," he kept saying.

"Do you really think I can?" I would ask in a trembling voice.

"I'm positive," he would firmly reply.

Within a month after learning Lloyd was dying from cancer, I watched him deteriorate physically to the point where he became as dependent as a baby. I bathed him, fed him, dressed him, and gave him his medicine. During that time, I had no opportunity to work on my own independence. Lloyd was so ill and his needs were so great that I just had no time for anything else. I cared for him around the clock until he died in my arms less than five months after his cancer was diagnosed.

One week after Lloyd's death I was sitting alone in the dark. In one hour, I thought, it will have been exactly a week since Lloyd died. How can I ever live without him? He was my life. I felt that part of me had been cut off, leaving me raw and bleeding.

Just then, the phone rang. It was my friend, Lynda. She had lost her husband to cancer some time before. I recalled one Sunday as Lloyd and I watched her drive away from church, completely alone. "Can you imagine how Lynda must hurt?" I had remarked to Lloyd. Now, of course, I knew how Lynda had felt. That night Lynda and I talked for two hours. It was such a comfort to talk to someone who had gone through what I was going through.

PASSING THE TEST

My biggest hurt has been my loneliness, my lack of companionship. Sometimes I pretend Lloyd is here and I talk to him a lot. This helps soothe the pain. Each morning I pray that God would help me get through the day, and that He would give me the strength and courage to live alone.

For a while, I felt Lloyd's death was totally unfair. I know now that such feelings are a normal part of the grief process—the "anger" phase. I looked back over our lives, and I thought, We've worked so hard. We've raised our children and planned for our future together. When I would see other couples, I felt angry and would think to myself, You don't know how lucky you are!

I recall one lady, during this time, coming to me and saying, "God never makes mistakes." I know she meant well, and I know that what she said is true, but it seemed so insensitive for her to say such a thing while my grief was so fresh. I couldn't help thinking, That's an easy thing for you to say—you still have your husband. The anger is a normal stage people go through after a loss, and God has helped me move beyond it.

One day, I received a check from Lloyd's place of employment. He had worked hard and had many certificates for perfect attendance. I thought to myself, I don't deserve this check, Lloyd does. I wonder what he would want me to spend it for? Then I had an idea.

About four months after Lloyd's death I took a giant step. I enrolled in a driver training course and paid for it with that check. Lloyd had asked me to do this and I wanted him to be proud of me. I remember thinking, I'm so terrified! But I can't let Lloyd down.

I didn't even know where the key went into the ignition. I didn't know the brake pedal from the accelerator. I had never noticed traffic lights or signs. I just rode along and Lloyd did it all. During those lessons I shook with fright. My mind would go blank at times. I kept praying, "Help me, God."

The day came for my driver's test. I asked my church friends for prayer. I felt completely inadequate. There was no way I could pass this test alone. I was shaking and so frightened. But . . .

I passed the test!

After the test, I said to the instructor, "I don't know how you feel about prayer, but that's what got me through this test." To me it was nothing less than a miracle from God.

My next test was to put my newfound skill to practical use by driving to church for the first time. I shook with fear as I slid behind the wheel. I had no confidence in my ability. Suddenly God brought these words to my mind, "I can do everything through [Christ] who gives me strength" (Philippians 4:13). That gave me courage to turn the key, press the accelerator, and move out into traffic. Shaking so badly I could hardly grip the steering wheel, I carefully urged and nudged that car all the way to church. Car and driver arrived in one piece.

That morning, I went to the eight-year-olds' Sunday school class where Lynda taught, and where my granddaughter attended, to help out. At the end of the class, Lynda and all the children prayed that I would make it home safely. When I got into the car I prayed, "O God, please help me get home!" And He did.

On another day when I needed to drive and felt very frightened about it, I took a Bible verse from my promise box. It read, "As I was with Moses so will I be with you" (Joshua 1:5). I thought, What a wonderful promise, just what I need today. I never could have learned to drive without God's help. I am so grateful for the privilege of being able to drive to church, to the cemetery, to go for coffee and to the grocery store. I feel comforted whenever I sit in the driver's seat, where Lloyd used to sit. I hope Lloyd can see me, and that he knows I can now get myself to church and to the doctor. I'm sure he's proud of me.

MY STRENGTH

Throughout my ordeal of grief, my friend Helen has phoned me many times. "How are you?" she would say. "Keep trusting God. You'll make it, Alice. I've had to give up my husband and my only daughter, but God helped me through that, and He will help you too. I am praying for you."

Friends like Helen and Lynda were my lifeline.

I developed a close friendship with Lynda. She phoned, took me places, and sent me lovely cards. She must have prayed before sending them because each one spoke to a need I had. Many days I felt overwhelmed with grief, yet I knew even before going to the mailbox that there would be a card from Lynda. I still have every one of them stacked up in the head of my bed. I am comforted as I read them again and again.

God has given me a peace I never believed I could have. I never imagined that I could stay alone at night and sleep well. I never even liked staying alone while Lloyd was at work. I always felt insecure and unsafe until he came home. But since Lloyd's death, God has given me such a sense of security and of His presence that I have not been afraid one night since being alone.

I find comfort in looking forward to heaven and being with Lloyd again. And I find great joy in the relationships with the children that we brought into the world together and who are a continuing part of Lloyd, living on after his departure.

I might not have come back to Sunday school if it were not for my granddaughter. She has special needs and going with her to help her gave me a purpose for attending. It also offered me an alternative to sitting alone in my adult Sunday School class (how I dreaded that!). Before he died, Lloyd asked me to look after our granddaughter. He loved her deeply and was very concerned about her future, so I have tried to help her any way I could—and doing so has been good therapy for me. In fact, I've found that helping others is the best thing I can do to help ease my own pain.

Living alone has made me depend on God more than ever. My suggestion to anyone else who is going through grief is to draw as close to God as you can. God is my strength. He has enabled me to accomplish things I never would have attempted while Lloyd was alive. I miss my husband and look forward to seeing him again in heaven.

There are challenges every day, but with God's help, I know I will make it.

HE LEADETH ME

In pastures green? Not always, sometimes He
Who knoweth best, in kindness leadeth me
In many ways where heavy shadows be.
Out of the sunshine warm and soft and bright—
Out of the sunshine into the darkest night;
I oft would faint with sorrow and affright;
So whether in the green or desert land
I trust although I may not understand.

And by still water? No, not always so;
Oftimes the heavy tempests round me blow,
And o'er my soul the waters and billows go,
But when the storms beat loudest and I cry
Aloud for help, the Master standeth by
And whispers to my soul, "Lo, it is I."
Above the tempest wild I hear Him say,
"Beyond this darkness lies a perfect day.
In every path of thine I lead the way."

So whether on the hilltops high and fair
I dwell, or in the sunless valleys where
The shadows lie—what matters? He is there.
So where He leads me, I can safely go.
And in the blest hereafter I shall know
Why in His wisdom, He hath led me so.

—Rev. John F. Chaplain

Dannie and I nursed together in the hospital many years ago. She was caring and grandmotherly with a gentle manner and a warm smile.

Her son had a long list of accomplishments back in the days when it was much harder and less common for a black person to succeed.

One summer afternoon Dannie phoned from her hospital bed and asked me to come and pray with her. Her son had been murdered.

5

Dannie's Story:
LOVE ... POURED OUT
FROM A BROKEN HEART

The LORD is my shepherd,
I shall not be in want.
He makes me lie down in green pastures,
he leads me beside quiet waters,
he restores my soul.

Psalm 23:1-2

I wonder why Buddy isn't answering his phone, I thought, walking the short distance from my front door to the back door of my son's home. I hope he hasn't fallen. Buddy had struggled with multiple sclerosis for twenty-three years—about half of his life. The last twelve of those years he had been confined to a wheelchair.

It was early morning and I was surprised to see all the lights in the house on and the television running. I hurried down the hall looking for my son, checking in different rooms. "Buddy," I called. "What's wrong, Buddy?"

He didn't answer.

Then I saw him. At first, my mind refused to comprehend what my eyes were seeing. He was lying on the floor with dried blood covering much of his head. A telephone cord was pulled tightly around his neck and in his chest were two stab wounds.

I seemed to go numb everywhere but in my heart. There, I felt a terrible, piercing pain. This couldn't be true! It just couldn't be true!

I fell down on my knees beside him."Oh, son," I said dazedly, "someone has killed you."

My next words were a desperate plea to the only One I knew who could help me at a time like this. "Oh, Lord," I said aloud, "give me strength to get up and find help." He answered my prayer. I don't know how I could have walked back to my house without God's strength. Once in my house, I phoned 911.

After reporting Buddy's murder to the police, I turned my face to heaven and prayed, "Oh God, please help me not to hate the people who killed my son."

Ruth Sissom recalls:

Those words describe Dannie's last impressions of her son, her only child. She never saw him after that, not even a viewing at the funeral home. Dannie, who was 81, had been experiencing heart problems for years, and the shock caused her heart condition to worsen, so that she had to be hospitalized.

A couple of days later my phone rang. I hadn't heard about the murder, and I didn't recognize the voice at first, but the caller sounded weak and troubled. "Ruth," said the voice, "somebody murdered my son. I'm in the hospital and they won't let me leave. Will you come to the hospital and pray for me?" Suddenly I recognized it as Dannie's voice. I first met Dannie when we worked as nurses at the same hospital many years before. It had been a couple years since I had talked to Dannie, so I wasn't expecting to get a call from her.

"Of course, I'll come," I replied. "I'll be there soon."

At the hospital, I sat on the edge of Dannie's bed with my arm around her. The entire bed shook with her uncontrollable sobs. Her heart was shattered, and she needed to express all her questions and feelings:

"How could anyone do such a terrible thing to a defenseless man in a wheelchair?" she wondered in anguish. "If only he could have fought back. He was so defenseless. He was kind and always helping others. He helped many young folks by paying them to cut the grass, run errands, or work in his adult foster care home. If those who murdered him needed money, they only had to ask him. He would have loaned it to them or given them a job to earn it. It hurts so much to think that he couldn't even defend himself."

"I FEEL SO ALONE."

Buddy was a special man, and Dannie had every right to be proud of him. A hard worker, Buddy had received a Master's Degree back in the days when it was much harder and less common for a black person to obtain one. He was the first black to be elected commissioner in his county. He spoke before school groups and was a great motivator and encourager of young people. Buddy had continued working, managing an adult foster care home, even though confined in a wheelchair by MS. Despite being weakened by his disease, he had never surrendered to it.

Having reached his middle-aged years, Buddy was preparing to retire. The MS had robbed him of much of his strength and his ability to walk, but it had not robbed him of his enthusiasm for life and his love for people. He continued to work, to be active in his community, and to be involved in helping other people. But suddenly, someone had done to him what the disease had failed to do: someone had robbed Buddy of his life.

The doctor wouldn't release Dannie from the hospital to go to the funeral; she was too ill. Months later, she recalled, "I wanted desperately to see my son once more so I wouldn't remember him like I found him that horrible morning. Now, every time I close my eyes I still see him as I found him that day. The people responsible for his death are in jail. I want to go see them, but it's not allowed. I wouldn't be mean to them. I would just ask them how they could possibly have done such a terrible thing to another human being."

Looking back over her ongoing process of grief, Dannie says, "My pain is so deep. I can't hold back the tears. Even now, I still cry a lot. And some people just do not understand. One person asked me why I was still wallowing in my grief. But she's not a mother. She can't possibly understand what it's like to lose your child. Buddy was my only child, and now I have no one to care for me in my old age. I was hospitalized many times and Buddy always made sure I had what I needed, even though he was in a wheelchair. He built me a house on his property so he could be sure I was safe and cared for. After his death, I never returned to my home. I just couldn't go back there. I feel so alone."

"THE REASON IS GOD."

I visited Dannie recently, and she is still kind and helpful to everyone she meets. She asked me to drive her to a nursing home to see a lady who had suffered a stroke. At the home she had a kind word for everyone—employees, patients in wheelchairs, people in the halls. She shook their hands and patted them on the shoulder. She tenderly cleaned out the mouth and moistened the lips of the lady we had come to see.

When we arrived back at Dannie's apartment, her phone rang. It was an elderly man in her building. His family lived too far away to visit often, so Dannie often washed his clothes and checked on him in his family's absence. I knew her heart was aching and yet she had found a key to grief recovery: Reach out and find others who are lonely or hurting, and minister to their needs.

I asked Dannie, "How are you doing in your recovery from the grief? And what would you encourage other people to do when they are going through grief?"

"I'm doing well," she responded, "so well, in fact, that my doctor can't believe it! The reason is God. My godson prayed with me every night for awhile after Buddy's death. That helped a lot. When I can't sleep I get up and read my Bible. Sometimes I feel like I can't pray and I don't really want to read my Bible, but I try anyway. I carry a Bible in my purse so I can have God's Word with me at all times. It comforts me. I read Psalm 23 again and again, and when I feel that terrible loneliness coming over me, I repeat the first words, 'The Lord is my Shepherd.'

"I also find comfort in songs. I love the song that says, 'He's brought me a mighty long way,' and the one that says, 'He never leaves me alone.'

"I'm always glad when people phone or visit me. It takes my mind off my sadness. When I'm alone it's worse. Many times I go to the grocery store or to other places where people are, so I won't be home alone.

"My relationship with God was good before all this happened. It is still good—maybe even closer than before. God has brought me through this terrible tragedy. He's still bringing me through it. He has given me strength, and I'm trusting in Him to go with me and help me in the days ahead."

....

NO, NEVER ALONE

I've seen the lightning flashing,
And heard the thunder roll,
I've felt sin's breakers dashing,
Which tried to conquer my soul,
I've heard the voice of my Savior,
He bids me still fight on,
He promised never to leave me,
Never to leave me alone.
No, never alone,
No, never alone,
He promised never to leave me,
Never to leave me alone.

—Author unknown

June learned firsthand that God can use disappointment, thwarted plans, and dashed dreams to carry out His perfect plan in the lives of His children.

6

June's Story:
Alzheimer's ...
and God's Perfect Plan

" ... Because God has said,
'Never will I leave you;
Never will I forsake you.'"

Hebrews 13:5

"You must have John admitted to a nursing home. You cannot stay up night and day to care for him."

I knew the doctor was right, but how could I ever live with the guilt of deserting my husband of forty-seven years? His Alzheimer's disease didn't change my love for him, or my marriage vows: "in sickness and in health, till death do us part." It was true I was worn out physically and emotionally from the strain of caring for John during the last eight years as his condition deteriorated. To complicate matters, John was diagnosed with cancer and was recovering from having his esophagus rebuilt. The doctor said he probably would not live longer than six months.

I made the only decision that could be made, and had John transferred from the hospital to the nursing home. The fact that the decision was inevitable didn't make it any less awful. I went home and cried all evening.

"THERE IS NOTHING WRONG WITH MY BRAIN!"

Our relationship as husband and wife had been over for several years. John was now more like my child than my husband. Putting him in a nursing home seemed like the final death sentence. My husband was now gone forever!

As I lay there in the stillness I imagined how John would feel to have strangers caring for him. He couldn't possibly understand what was really happening; he surely would think I abandoned him. I knew how to care for him better than anyone else. Even though I was absolutely helpless to change the situation, I felt an enormous load of guilt for letting him down.

In the days that followed, I reflected on our life together. We had five wonderful children, and they were a great joy to me. I thought about how God had led us through a series of circumstances which helped to prepare us specifically for John's illness.

Some twenty years earlier, John and I had become interested in foreign missionary work. We were friends of Dr. Rhodes, a medical missionary who was stationed at Ippy Hospital in the Central African Republic. I knew a couple of nurses there and how short-staffed they were. I wanted to become a nurse and go to help them in God's work. John had worked in the power-house of a large company for many years. He possessed skills that were desperately needed at Ippy. We talked with Dr. Rhodes and he recommended us to his mission board. We were accepted, and would start work at Ippy in two years—which meant I had two years in which to become a qualified nurse. There wasn't a two-year registered nurse program available at that time, so I took licensed practical nurse training.

By the time I became an LPN, our two year limit had expired; so John and I renewed our application. There were medical tests required that revealed a problem with John's EEG (a brain wave test). He was required to have a total medical workup to confirm that he did not have a medical problem that would hinder his work on the mission field. John was terribly upset over this development.

"There is nothing wrong with my brain," he flatly declared. "I am not crazy." He refused the total work-up. At first it appeared that I had gone to nursing school in vain. Our dreams of missionary work were dashed. Later we learned that John had Alzheimer's disease and we realized that God had hindered our going to Africa because it would have devastated John.

Alzheimer's patients cannot adapt to new situations; they can't deal with stress. It was definitely best for us to stay home. But it was difficult for me to accept. I had completed nurses' training and was excited about serving God in Africa. I found that the first purpose for my nursing knowledge was to care for my own husband. Because I understood the disease process, I could better cope with the repetitiveness, his continual wandering, and at the same time I knew how important it was to preserve his dignity.

As John's condition worsened I had to take on more of the responsibility of running our home. John had handled our finances. I had never written a check or paid the bills. I had a dreadful time at first. It seemed my check-book never balanced and bills were often paid late. Fortunately I have a son who is a CPA and he bailed me out many times. It seemed like forever, but I finally mastered my little corner of the confusing world of finance.

Now with John in the nursing home, large bills began coming and straining my budget. John outlived his six months predicted life span. I knew I had to find a way to make some money to pay for his care. So I began praying, "Lord, help me find a job." It had been thirteen years since I had been employed, but I began job hunting. Soon I discovered a second purpose for my LPN training. I could earn a much better wage as a nurse than in an unskilled position and would be able to pay for John's care. I visited a nursing home and was surprised to find a woman I knew working there. The home looked clean and the patients appeared well cared for. I prayed about it and felt a peace about accepting a nursing position ...

But I was so frightened!!

"IT'S OKAY TO LEAVE US."

Nursing care had changed dramatically since I had worked. At first I thought I would lose my mind. How could I ever learn and perform all that was expected of me? It seemed my mind had shut down while coping with John's Alzheimer's disease. The way I had preserved my sanity was to ignore much of what was going on and to simply concentrate completely on caring for him. I also had to program out much of John's confusing speech in order to survive from day to day. I lived in sort of a cocoon and my thinking processes became very dulled.

Now, faced with the awesome responsibility of providing health-care to other people, I drew comfort and strength from the hymn, "Be Still My Soul, The Lord is on Thy Side." My employer patiently worked with me and gradually, over a period of about six months, I began to feel confident and competent. I began to realize how much I enjoyed older people. God gave me a special love for them.

Over those months, John became weaker. Nearly two years after his first bout with cancer, he was diagnosed with liver cancer. He needed around-the-clock care. He was admitted to the nursing home where I worked on Tuesday. The following Saturday was my day off. I phoned to ask how he was.

"He has been quite restless all afternoon," the nurse told me.

I decided to go and spend some time with him. For two hours, I was at his bedside, reading the Bible to him. He seemed to settle down while I read God's Word. Then I talked to him and told him it was okay to leave us. That he would be with the Lord, and the children and I would be fine. God would continue to care for me as He had cared for us as a family for forty-nine years. I prayed with him, then came home and shed buckets of tears.

The next day the nurse phoned. "John is worse," she said. "You had better come."

I rushed to the nursing home, but as I arrived, the nurse said, "I'm sorry, June. He died just five minutes ago."

I felt a mixture of sadness and relief. John's suffering was finally over. In the days following his death, God strengthened and comforted me through His Word, through my family, and my church friends.

My biggest problem since John's death has been the terrible loneliness. After forty-nine years of marriage I feel like half of me is gone. I pray a great deal and read the Bible for strength to cope with each day. During the first year I felt a lot of anger toward God, John, and family members who didn't accept John's illness and didn't support me in caring for him. A lot of resentment had built up inside me over the years.

I found it very therapeutic to write a letter expressing all the things I felt angry about. I put it away and one week later I read it again. I thought, All this anger should not be part of my life. I prayed, "Oh God, forgive me and help me to forgive others." I tore the letter up and God gave me peace and release from the anger.

Looking back, glimpsing God's plan

The thing that has helped me most is knowing that God has a perfect plan for my life even though I don't understand it all. I am more aware of my complete dependence on Him. I've asked Him to give me a positive attitude and cheerful outlook on life. Psalm 46 has been my mainstay, especially verses 1 and 10: "God is our refuge and strength, an ever present help in trouble. . . . Be still, and know that I am God."

God has given me opportunities to use my experiences for the good of others. I've ministered to families of patients who have died at the nursing home. I've been able to help them deal with their anger and other emotions related to their losses. Out of my own painful experience, I've been able to help other people weigh the decision to put a loved one in a nursing home.

Someone once said that life is best lived looking forward, and best understood looking backward. I've found that to be absolutely true. Looking back over my life, I can see God's leading in ways I couldn't see in the midst of my confusing circumstances:

How He kept us from going to Africa which would have been a disaster for John.

How He prepared me to care for John and pay for his care by leading me through nurses' training.

How He prepared me to have a beneficial impact on other lives by taking the lessons of my painful experiences and turning them into helpful counsel for others who face the same decisions and issues.

A favorite hymn of mine is "All The Way My Savior Leads Me." I'm constantly surprised at all the ways He provides for me, protects me and shows me His love. Adversity really can bring us close to God. When we reach bottom we learn to exist each day by His strength as we read His Word and pray.

He truly is a great God!

....

ALL THE WAY MY SAVIOR LEADS ME

All the way my Savior leads me
    What have I to ask beside?
Can I doubt His tender mercy,
    Who through life has been my Guide?

Heavenly peace, divinest comfort,
    Here by faith in Him to dwell!
For I know, whate're befall me,
    Jesus doeth all things well.

—Fanny J. Crosby

"For her sake I must not withdraw and become drowned in my loneliness," says John as he copes with the loss of his loving wife of thirty-five years. "She would not want it that way. So I count my blessings."

7

John's Story:
MY PLACE OF SHELTER

The LORD will be a refuge for his people.

Joel 3:16

The phone rang at 6:00 a.m., just as I expected. It would be Betty, my wonderful wife of 35 years, calling from her hospital bed. We both anticipated the following day when, according to the doctors, she would be able to come home.

I picked up the receiver and listened for her voice—but the voice was not Betty's. My heart sank and a heavy feeling of dread and panic gripped me. I heard the nurse saying, "Your wife's condition has suddenly changed. Please come to the hospital right away."

"Oh no, oh no," was all I could say as I drove to the hospital in a daze. On the way, I reflected on our life together.

REFLECTIONS ABOUT BETTY

We enjoyed an excellent relationship and truly delighted in each other. Each day when I finished work I hurried home to Betty. I couldn't get home fast enough to be with the one I loved. Everyone else loved Betty too. She was positive, friendly, and always helping others.

I thought back to nine years before when she had undergone cancer surgery. For about four months I drove her daily to the hospital for radiation treatments. Those were difficult days as the chemotherapy made Betty very ill. What a relief when that was finally behind us. Our last seven happy years were interrupted by occasional trips to the hospital for blood transfusions. Then she would feel better and resume her usual activities.

Recently she was feeling exhausted even with the job she loved, manager of the school cafeteria. She went right to bed when she came home from work each day. The weakness increased and she could not regain her strength.

The doctor admitted her to the hospital for tests and treatments. Then he gave us the horrible news, "The cancer has spread to her bone marrow. She will not recover from this. However, she is well enough to be discharged." I could not even imagine living without her. I tried to ignore the dreadful news and focused instead on how good it would be to have her home again. When I left Betty the night before, I had said, "I'll see you tomorrow and the next day I'll take you home."

I hurried into the hospital, anxiously reflecting on what the nurse had said. What did she mean by a "sudden change" in Betty's condition? Would she be awake and know me?

A DREADFUL DECISION

A deep pain pierced my heart as I viewed the shocking scene in Betty's room. Tubes were everywhere; a machine was breathing for her and she was not responsive. It seemed like a horrible dream.

I phoned our four grown children, and they were stunned that their mother could have become so ill so suddenly. They came right away.

The nurse gathered us together and explained. "This morning Betty seemed fine. She asked about another patient who had open heart surgery.

She was concerned and had been praying for her. Suddenly Betty's vital signs took a life-threatening plunge. We started all our emergency procedures, but she has not regained consciousness."

Then the doctor came in and informed us that there was nothing more that could be done. The children and I had to decide how long to leave her on life support. It was a dreadfully agonizing decision, but within a few hours we all agreed not to keep her alive on machines when there was no hope of recovery. Within a couple of minutes after the respirator was turned off she was gone.

I felt as if I were in a dazed stupor. I couldn't believe my precious wife was not coming home. The doctors said she could come home tomorrow. This made no sense, no sense at all.

GETTING THROUGH THE GRIEF

Somehow I made it through the shock, confusion, and busyness of the next few days. Words of comfort seemed totally inadequate during the initial stages of grief. Nothing anyone said could really cut through my shock and pain and make a difference. What helped was the presence of caring people who were willing to share my sorrow.

Even Scripture can seem harsh at first. My family, church family, and friends understood what I was going through and they were absolutely wonderful to me. They showed their love by being with me, listening as I poured out my grief, by bringing food to our home, and helping with practical details. One act of love that was especially healing for me was when they expressed their affection for Betty and told me of the many loving ways she had touched their lives.

I've never felt angry at God, but I still ask, "Why?" I know there is a reason for all the situations God allows in our lives, but I do wonder why Betty and I were not allowed to grow old together. I realize I may not know the answer this side of heaven.

Adjusting to life without Betty has been the toughest struggle of my life. The hardest thing of all is being alone in the house. Everywhere I look, I see her things—her clothes, her jewelry, the afghan she crocheted on the sofa. My way of coping has been to stay away from home as much as possible. I leave early for work and in the evening I drive around, visit my dad in the nursing home, and go to a restaurant. I purposely arrive home late so I can go right to bed. At night I cry a lot.

I've thought how grief might be different for a man than for a woman when a spouse dies. I've concluded that the feelings may be much the same for both, but we have different places of shelter—havens where we feel safeguarded from the constant stabs of grief.

For the woman that place of shelter may be her home or place of employment, the place where she feels most comfortable in her familiar routines and surroundings. It may be more difficult in her husband's domain—

the garage, workshop, barn, or his place of employment. These places can contain many painful reminders of the loss of the man she loved.

For a man—at least for me—my place of shelter is anywhere but the house. Everywhere I look in that house, I see Betty's things. It is her domain—the place she was part of; the place she cared for with love and tenderness. I see her everywhere I look. I see her laughing, talking, sleeping, preparing meals, cleaning, washing clothes, and waiting to greet me after a busy day at work. The house seems like a huge empty tomb without her. The loneliness and sadness become overwhelming if I stay in the house very long. I just have to get outside to my place of shelter. That shelter is anywhere other than home—even though home was once the happiest spot on earth for me. How thankful we can be that the Lord is a Shelter and a Refuge for those who trust in Him—a far safer, more secure Shelter than any walled fortress on earth.

SALT IN MY WOUNDS

It amazes me to see other widowers who have lost their wives of many years, yet who never seem to unravel emotionally. I'm dealing with uncontrollable tears and deep stabs of emotional pain. I wonder if some are able to put on a mask of apparent indifference and strength in public, and do their real grieving behind closed doors. It seems to me that to have loved deeply is to grieve deeply.

When waves of sadness wash over me, I feel I'm about to be swept away into despair, drowned in my sorrow. At those times, I think of what Betty used to say and it cheers me—at least a little. She used to kid me when I didn't get my way and say, "Come on, let's go and have a pity party." For her sake, I make a deliberate decision, day after day, not to get drawn into a pity party. I refuse to withdraw into isolation. Betty wouldn't want it that way.

Instead, I try to count my blessings. I have wonderful children and a caring church family. I realize how blessed I am when I meet other widowers who have no one. They either have no family or a family that does not seem to care or show love.

The amount of grief I see in this world is unbelievable. There is always someone worse off than we are, so I look around for others to help. Staying busy leaves less lonely time. I'm better now at recognizing needs of others and find that it works best to just quietly do things without asking first or making a big deal of it. There are many lonely people who just need someone to be friendly to them. That's something I can do.

I've had experiences I have not shared with others for fear they would question my sanity. However, I understand that these are common grief experiences for spouses who have shared a close, lengthy relationship like Betty and I enjoyed. Once I "saw" her face in the window. On another occasion, I had a dream in which she was so real I felt I could reach out and touch her. The dream took place in a shopping mall, and after the dream I actually went to the mall and sat, watching all the people, hoping Betty would come along. I know she won't, she can't, it's impossible—yet a part of me still hopes she will come home again.

When I'm riding in the truck I feel close to her because we went many places together in our truck. At times I've lost touch with reality. I have been driving my truck and I've lost track of where I was going. All of a sudden I would realize I had gone past where I should have turned. I am so preoccupied with my grief and the stresses of adjustment to life without Betty that it's easy to forget where I am or what I am doing. Just when I think I'm making progress in recovering from the grief, the sadness will suddenly roll over me again like a huge wave.

It's difficult to go places alone. A painful experience is to go to a restaurant and be asked by the greeter, "Are you alone?" or "How many?" when it is evident I am by myself. It feels like another spoonful of salt being poured into my raw wounds of grief. I never sit in a restaurant at a table for two. I feel a deep ache in my heart as I look at that other empty chair where Betty should be. Instead, I sit at a table with four chairs. Somehow it lessens the pain a little. When my friends invite me to go on outings or out to dinner, my first inclination is to refuse and spare myself the pain of going alone. But I know Betty would want me to make the effort, so increasingly I try to accept. It is getting easier as time goes on.

KEEPING TRADITIONS ALIVE

My children have been super. They help in many ways. They do my washing and cook for me. They write my checks and keep my checkbook balanced.

Betty did all the check writing—and there's a story behind that. At one time I had my own checkbook, but I could never keep it up to date and balanced. Finally, Betty said, "Let's close your checkbook, and I'll write all the checks!" She was an organized record keeper. She served as treasurer of the church missions committee. I was glad to let her handle our finances. The checkbook still baffles me. When I run short of money I write a check and leave a note for my daughters so they can keep the account current. I am so thankful for their patience with me.

Every Sunday, Betty and I invited our children with their families to our home for dinner. They could bring as many friends as they wished and we always had enough food and room for all. We loved having our home filled with happy family chatter and laughter. I knew Betty would want us to continue this family tradition, so each Saturday evening I still peel vegetables and start the preparation. My daughters do the cooking on Sunday and we spend a happy time together. One of my ten grandchildren usually spends the afternoon. We go to church and out for a treat after the service. If I need a quick date, my thirteen year old granddaughter is available. She is a great encouragement to me.

I remind my children that life is fragile. They should never leave each other angry or go to sleep at night mad at each other. They should never go to work or leave each other for any reason without saying good-bye. We must make the most of today because we have no promise of tomorrow.

I find myself longing to go home to heaven more than I ever did before. I have precious treasures there and it seems more real to me. I'm looking forward most of all to being with Betty. I know the most wonderful thing about heaven will be seeing and being with Christ. But now, while we are separated, I long most of all to be with my loved ones again. Meanwhile, I concentrate on all the happy times we had together.

Memory is a wonderful gift. I have so many cherished remembrances of our lives together. God blessed me with a loving, virtuous wife and I see her pictured in the following excerpts from Proverbs 31:

> A wife of noble character who can find?
>   She is worth far more than rubies.
> Her husband has full confidence in her
>   and lacks nothing of value.
> She brings him good, not harm,
>   all the days of her life. . . .
> She gets up while it is still dark;
> she provides food for her family
>   and portions for her servant girls. . . .
> She opens her arms to the poor
>   and extends her hands to the needy. . . .
> She is clothed with strength and dignity;
>   she can laugh at the days to come.
> She speaks with wisdom,
>   and faithful instruction is on her tongue.
> She watches over the affairs of her household
>   and does not eat the bread of idleness.
> Her children arise and call her blessed;
>   her husband also, and he praises her. . . .
> Give her the reward she has earned,
>   and let her works bring her praise at the city gate.

I found the following poem in Betty's Bible. It was apparently comforting to her as she grew weaker and anticipated heaven. It has become comforting to me as I think about the compassion of God for sparing her from further suffering.

....

GOD'S GARDEN

> God saw her getting tired,
>   When a cure was not to be,
> He clasped His hand around her,
>   And whispered, "Come to me."

She didn't deserve what she went through
   And so He gave her rest;
God's garden must be beautiful,
   For He only takes the best.

At peace in God's beautiful garden,
   Away from sorrow and pain,
Someday when life's journey has ended,
   You'll all be together again.

God was watching from above,
   And knew she had her share,
He gently closed her weary eyes
   And took her in His care.

The golden gates stand open,
   He knew she needed rest.
God's garden must be beautiful
   He always takes the best.

—Author unknown

The doctor said five years, but instead, it was only three months after lymphoma was diagnosed that Bonnie lost her loving husband of almost twenty-six years.

In the following pages, she shares her intense struggle with loneliness, and relates how she is turning to God for companionship.

8

Bonnie's Story:
LOVE IN A DIFFERENT WAY

I can do everything through [Christ]
who gives me strength.

Philippians 4:13

It was the middle of the night. I was roused from a deep sleep to a state of drowsy semiconsciousness. Then, rolling over in bed, I reached out to touch my husband ...

But he was gone!

Suddenly I was wide awake. The horrible reality that my husband was not there rolled over me like a huge ocean wave, drowning me in loneliness. I longed to have him hold me in his arms and I yearned to feel the warmth of his embrace. I longed to hear him say as he had so many times, "Everything is going to be all right." But he was gone and he was never coming back.

Uncontrollable sobs began shaking my entire body.

Bill and I began dating in junior high school, and for nearly twenty-six years we shared a loving marriage relationship. He was my best friend. He loved me just the way I was and he understood me. As I lay, engulfed in my loneliness, I started reliving the events that had culminated in his death.

"PLEASE, GOD, DON'T TAKE MY HUSBAND!"

Bill was the encourager in our relationship. He always saw a bright tomorrow coming.

But a time came when his usual cheery optimism began to fade. He told me he was feeling tired and becoming concerned about his health. He had episodes of weakness at work. One day, he passed out and I had to go pick him up at work and bring him home. As we left his place of employment, he said, "I have a strange feeling that I'll never come back here."

He sank into severe discouragement as he became more concerned about his physical condition. I finally convinced him to take a medical leave. This gloomy behavior was not like him. He had always been my encourager, but now I was preoccupied with encouraging Bill. I fixed foods I thought he would especially enjoy. "Nothing tastes good to me," was his response.

Bill underwent medical testing. At first medication was suspected as the cause of Bill's illness. Then tuberculosis was suggested. Then a rare exotic disease.

One night, I dreamed that Bill had died and I was crying uncontrollably. I shared this dream with a friend, and she reminded me it was only a dream. Still, I felt something was terribly wrong. Finally exploratory surgery was recommended. Bill's response was, "Once they do surgery, I'm gone." But we had to do something; he was becoming weaker each day.

It was Christmas Eve when I received the dreadful news from the doctor. "It's cancer—lymphoma."

I looked the doctor straight in the eye and asked, "Is my husband going to die?"

"Medical science can do many things today," he replied. "In Bill's case, there is an eighty to one hundred percent chance of success with chemotherapy."

"And if the chemotherapy isn't successful," I asked, "how long can I expect to have my husband?"

"We're talking probably five years."

Five years! In five years I might not have my husband! I was stunned. I went home and prayed through my tears, "Please, God, don't take my husband!"

How can I go on?

Bill was very frightened of chemotherapy. It was unlike him to be so upset. He always had a calm "wait and see" attitude. His mother had died of cancer two years before and the vivid memories of her weighed heavily on his decision. Finally he agreed.

I felt God was directing me to take time off to be with Bill. So I took a month off and went with him for the treatments. He was so weak that he had to lean on my shoulders in order to walk from the bedroom to the living room where he stayed all day. He listened to Christian music to help pass the weary time. I thank God for allowing us that month together. It was a precious time.

The evening of the first day I returned to work, I had to take Bill to the emergency room. The next day they put him on a respirator and gave him medication to relax him. He never opened his eyes again.

My favorite song of comfort was "Peace in the Midst of the Storm." I put the tape player beside Bill's bed and played that song hoping he could hear it with me. I stayed with him twenty-four hours a day for the fourteen days until he died—just three months after the cancer was diagnosed. I had expected that at the very least we would have five years together. I could not believe it was over! How could I ever go on without him?

After Bill died, several well-meaning people said such things as, "It was Bill's time to go," or, "Don't be sad, he's in heaven now," or, "God knows best." Those comments seemed so unfeeling and lacking in understanding of what I was going through. A person who is still in the shock of grief is simply not emotionally prepared to say, "Yes, I'm sure things are really much better now that my loved one is gone." People who have suffered a fresh loss should be allowed to grieve, to work through their pain at their own rate, and to heal at their own rate.

"I don't care if I live or die."

As I write these words, it has been nearly three years since Bill's death. There is a deep ache in my heart that never leaves. It has been extremely difficult as I've tried to adjust to life without him. I have the feeling I'm not a whole person anymore. Part of me seems to be missing. I realize I'm sometimes left out of social functions because I am not a couple.

One of the most difficult adjustments for me has been parenting without him. I feel gypped at times. I have even asked God, "Why did you take Bill when I need him to help me with our children?" Our oldest daughter was married and seemed to cope best with her dad's death. Bill was with her during labor when our granddaughter was born. Now she is expecting again, and though she has a wonderful, supportive husband, she feels cheated as she approaches the birth without her dad's reassurance.

A sadness still hovers over us at holiday time. All the children have expressed the feeling, "It isn't fair! Why does a good man like Dad have to die?" Sometimes we said angry words to each other. We were all hurting and in my pain I sometimes did not deal effectively with the children.

One day, I didn't bother getting dressed until 3:00 p.m. This is totally unlike me. I told God that day, "I don't care if I live or die." I felt completely overwhelmed. I just sat around all day, cried, and ate. When I feel unable to cope it is easy to give in to the temptation to eat to soothe my pain. One thing I had promised myself after Bill died was that I was going to lose weight. I did really well for a while. One day I went to the weight loss clinic to weigh in. It had been a bad week and I had put on a few extra pounds. The lady there confirmed my weight gain.

"Have you thought about counseling?" she asked.

I wanted to scream at her. I felt like saying, "Let me tell you what I'm going through. You have no idea what it is like to be a single parent while dealing with the death of your spouse!" Then I felt guilty for feeling angry at her.

My children and I have learned through this experience and are still growing. Through the help of God, advice and counsel from my patient pastor, and the prayers and support of family and friends, we have weathered the storm. I am learning to lean on God more. I keep praying, "Lord, help me to react properly in a calm manner." I'm learning to trust God for one day at a time and sometimes from one moment to the next.

I meditate often on Philippians 4:13: "I can do everything through [Christ] who gives me strength." God gives me courage and confidence through that verse.

I can look back and see how God prepared me for this time. He provided a good job for me several years before Bill's illness, so I would be able to provide for myself after he was gone. I had almost quit my job several years before Bill's death. I was feeling exhausted with the strain of my responsibilities at work, our family, and our church work. Bill and I had prayed about it and I had decided to give my notice. Then I felt a definite leading from God not to quit. He knew what was ahead. I'm glad I obeyed Him.

Bill and I were involved in children's ministries in the church. When we left that responsibility, we had to give up the house that was provided with the job. We rented a house for four years and then moved to a sub-level apartment. After Bill died that apartment seemed like a dungeon to me. I remember actually pounding on the walls. It was a way of releasing some of my frustration and pain. I never imagined I would own a home of my own, but God has provided me a nice home.

Since becoming a widow, I think of God as my husband as well as my Lord. Bill and I talked about everything. Now I'm learning to talk to God just like I did to Bill. I tell him about how tired I feel, or about my bad day at work. I admit to Him that I'm feeling frustrated or that I don't understand why all this has happened. My relationship with Him is closer than ever before.

I've learned to stay involved with other people. Though I often don't feel like it, I attend church functions and accept invitations for dinner with friends. When asked to participate in social functions, my first instinct was to say, "Don't you know I'm grieving? I don't want to go." But when I start withdrawing from others it becomes a downward spiral leading to depression. Now, when I feel "blue," I force myself to visit someone, go shopping, or phone and encourage someone else. I also enjoy sending cards to others who need cheering up. These activities help to pick me up.

I was once asked to sing in the choir. "No," I replied, "I can't sing without crying and I'll be embarrassed." But then I made myself do it and now I really enjoy singing. I teach third and fourth grade children in Sunday school, and I just love their enthusiasm.

God has given me opportunities to comfort others going through loss similar to mine. Sometimes this stirs up my hurt, but it also brings healing for my pain.

My biggest problem has been the lack of companionship and the feeling of loneliness and abandonment that accompanies it. Bill was always complimenting me. "You look pretty," or, "That dress looks so nice on you." Sometimes I think to myself, What's the use of trying to look nice? Who cares anyway?

Bill and I used to hold hands a lot—during a walk, while watching TV, or a meal times. I used to tease him and ask, "When I'm old and gray will you still hold my hand? Will you still open the car door for me?" We had planned on growing old together and it was so frightening to think I would have to grow old alone.

"If anything happens to me," Bill sometimes said, "I hope you can find someone else." I know there's no one I could ever love like I loved Bill. But Bill's grandmother—who was in a second marriage herself—once said to me, "You learn to love in a different way." Perhaps.

Being single again has been an extremely difficult adjustment. I don't think I will ever really get used to it. I find it difficult to meet the needs of my children for both a father and mother. I keep thinking that maybe God will allow me to meet a man who doesn't want his wife to work!

Meanwhile I have a peace knowing God loves me, that He has promised to supply my needs and I can totally depend on Him. My painful loneliness drives me to Him and I am comforted as I read His Word and talk to Him. He is so good to me and I praise Him each day as I journey onward in faith.

PEACE IN THE MIDST OF THE STORM

When the world that I've been living in collapses at my feet
When my life is shattered and torn
Though I'm windswept and battered, I can cling to His cross
And find peace in the midst of the storm.

There is peace in the midst of my storm tossed life;
Oh, there's an Anchor, there's a Rock to cast my faith upon
Jesus rides in my vessel so I fear no alarm,
He gives me peace in the midst of my storm!

—Steve Adams

Sharon joined a class I was teaching on Living Through Loss. When I met her, she was trembling and frightened. Previously married, she had become engaged to a wonderful man, and her happiness had seemed assured. Then the unthinkable had happened: her fiancé was murdered.

See how her struggle and her pain have been transformed into healing and help for other victims of violence.

9

Sharon's Story:
THE CROSS IN MY POCKET

LET GO AND LET GOD

As children bring their broken toys
With tears for us to mend,
I brought my broken dreams to God,
Because He was my Friend.

But then, instead of leaving Him
In peace, to work alone,
I hung around and tried to help,
With ways that were my own.

At last, I snatched them back and cried,
"How can you be so slow?"
"My child," He said, "What could I do?
You never did let go."

Author unknown

"I love you, Chuck."

"I love you, too, Sharon. I'll see you right after work this afternoon."

We were excited about our future together. Our wedding date was six months away. We shared a hug and he was gone. That was the last time I would feel the warmth of his embrace.

At the end of the day, Chuck didn't come as he had promised. He always kept his promises. He never kept me waiting without calling. Worried and uneasy, I drove to his shop. All the lights were on and his car was there. Something isn't right, I thought. I went next door and phoned the police.

The police arrived in a few minutes, and I entered the shop with the officers. We found Chuck's body in a huddle on the floor. He had been shot.

It sounds like a cliché to call an experience like this a "nightmare," but that's exactly what it was like. I felt fear and horror, mingled with a sense of unreality and dreamlike detachment. I could not believe this was really happening. How could all our wonderful dreams and plans be destroyed so suddenly? How could Chuck's life be over—just like that? How could I ever go on without him?

DEALING WITH ANGER

The day of Chuck's murder, I received another terrible shock. An acquaintance informed me that the police were asking people who knew me if I had any motive to kill Chuck! I couldn't believe that I could be a suspect! With all the pain I felt and the abysmal sense of loss over the deep love we had for each other, I found it unthinkable that anyone could suspect me of killing this wonderful man!

But I learned that this is normal. Whenever someone is murdered, the people closest to the victim usually become suspects. The police questioned me. They searched my car and my purse for a gun or other weapon. Even though I knew the police were just doing their job, I felt hurt, angry, and victimized all over again. They told me they would keep me informed about the case. Instead, I heard about it through others.

Two days after Chuck died, I was cleaning out his car. I was praying, "Oh, if only I could talk to him one more time!" All at once a song came on the car radio, "If Tomorrow Never Comes." I felt comforted by the words and believed it was a message from God to me.

As the days went by, my anger increased. I felt filled with a lust for revenge against the unknown person who had taken Chuck's life from him. And I also resented God for taking Chuck away.

Then the day came when the police announced a break in the investigation. A suspect had been apprehended. I saw him for the first time when I walked into the courtroom—and I felt like killing him.

At the same time, I also had thoughts of suicide. What was the use of going on living? I had lost my future husband and the family we had planned. The house we planned to live in was sold. The business that was to support us was sold. I was not his wife—only a fiancée—so I had no say in those decisions.

A neighbor told me about grief classes at a nearby church. I attended and joined a support group there. It helped me to learn that what I was feeling was normal after a tragic, violent death. I was without a job and felt humiliated at having to accept financial help. The church people were kind, understanding, and caring. They brought me groceries, took me to lunch, prayed for me and supported me during my job search, and celebrated with me when I found a job.

There are still times I feel resentful for the way my life has changed and my dreams have been stolen. But I keep reminding myself that I have a job and good health and I can pay my bills.

DEALING WITH LONELINESS

The loneliness is hard. Sometimes when I'm feeling really lonely, I take the last shirt Chuck wore and hold it close to me, and kiss it. Chuck had a pet cat he was very fond of, and I brought that cat home to live with me. It helps me to have something of Chuck's that I can love.

I've had to disregard a lot of things people say to me. About two months after Chuck's death, a woman said, "If you want to sell your engagement ring, I'd love to buy it." It stabbed deeply to even think of selling this important token of Chuck's love for me.

Chuck played the organ. He played love songs that expressed how he felt about me, and I miss hearing him play. We had selected our wedding songs. I planned to have Chuck play some of them on the organ and tape them to be played at the church on our wedding day. I had taped Chuck playing the organ with all the songs I loved, but I have not been able to find that tape. Many of my things were packed in boxes, ready to be unpacked at our future home. Someday I'll unpack those boxes, but I'm not ready to face that yet.

My daughter (from a previous marriage) and I have grown closer since Chuck's death. She listens to me, accepts my feelings, and shows she cares. On the first anniversary of Chuck's death, she was the only one who remembered. She took me out to dinner and bought me a dozen carnations. We spent the evening together. Those caring touches really help.

Friends from the church have been very kind. They took me to lunch, made phone calls, and sent letters and cards of encouragement that really picked me up. I start to cry just thinking of all the loving support I have received. It helped greatly to know there were people who cared that I was hurting and who wanted to help ease the pain. When you care about someone who is grieving, it's so important to keep those cards and phone calls coming regularly for the first year or two. A card on the anniversary of the death is comforting.

Another way I have been encouraged is by a kind neighbor who fixes things that break down around my house. Handyman help is really appreciated by women who live alone.

I have three poems that I keep on the refrigerator or table, and I read them often. They are: "Don't Quit," "Let Go and Let God," and "Footprints." Reading and rereading these poems gives me courage to go on.

THE CROSS IN MY POCKET

I was working at a nursing home after Chuck died and a nurse who also worked there gave me a card with a small wooden cross on it. There was a poem beside the cross that read:

THE CROSS IN MY POCKET

I carry a cross in my pocket
A simple reminder to me
Of the fact that I am a Christian
No matter where I may be.

This little cross is not magic
Nor is it a good luck charm
It isn't meant to protect me
From every physical harm.

It's not for identification
For all the world to see
It's simply an understanding
Between my Savior and me.

When I put my hand in my pocket
To bring out a coin or key
The cross is there to remind me
Of the price He paid for me.

It reminds me too, to be thankful
For my blessings day by day
And to strive to serve Him better
In all that I do and say.

It's also a daily reminder
Of the peace and comfort I share
With all who know my Master
And give themselves to His care.

So I carry a cross in my pocket
Reminding no one but me
That Jesus Christ is Lord of my life
If only I'll let Him be.

—Verna Thomas

When my heart would ache and I wondered if I could make it through the day, I would reach for that wooden cross in my pocket. It reminded me that God was with me, and He gave me the strength to keep going.

There are times I find it difficult to concentrate. I seem accident-prone, I feel short tempered, and I cry easily. It helps to tell my boss that a certain event is upsetting me, such as a court appearance or the anniversary of the death. She is more understanding if she is aware I am under a lot of stress.

I've discovered some resources and approaches to grief that have helped me work my way through the pain and sorrow:

Write a letter to your loved one. Tell him or her what you are feeling. I wrote what was on my own heart and read it at Chuck's memorial service. It helped me say to good-bye to him. I've saved that letter and I've read it over many times, and I always find it comforting. Here is what I wrote:

MY LOVE, MY FRIEND, MY HUSBAND-TO-BE, CHUCK

So many times each day I am reminded of you.
I do things that we did together.
I hear things that we heard together.
I see things that we saw together.
You initiated some feelings in me that helped open an
entirely new form of intensity in my life.
Why God chose to cross our paths when He did is still a miracle,
and why you had to leave, I don't understand.
It seems like so very long ago now that I held you in my arms,
but I know I have lived and loved a lifetime
in the short time we had together.

You were: My Love, My Friend, My Husband-to-Be, Chuck.

Reach out to someone for help, if you are having thoughts of suicide. Reach out to someone for help. Talk to a counselor or a pastor. Remember that the grief process is temporary and suicide is permanent.

Stay closely connected with God. Read daily devotional books like **Our Daily Bread.** Read your Bible, and talk to God daily.

Stay involved with people and with life. Talk to people. Take a class on grief recovery so you can understand what you are feeling and what is normal. In classes and support groups you can meet others who are struggling with loss and yet are making it. This gives you confidence.

Realize God has a reason for everything that happens to us. He didn't cause everything that happens, but He can use it to bring about something good.

Concentrate on things you can still be thankful for.

Treasure memories and mementos. Keep something that your loved one wore or valued. When you feel very lonely, then hold that memento close, cry in it, wear it. Some people make the mistake, in the most intense phases of their grief, of disposing of all reminders of their lost loved one, because reminders stir up pain. But ultimately, that pain becomes a healing twinge of melancholy rather than a stabbing pain. Mementos enable us to keep memories alive.

Put off major decisions (a job change, moving to a new house, and so forth) until your perspective becomes clearer. But make as many of your own day-to-day decisions as you can. Your friends or family members, trying to be helpful, may say, "Let's just get rid of this reminder," or, "You should do this and you shouldn't do that." Meaning well, they may make decisions on your behalf that you will regret later. Also, making everyday decisions helps to bring you back to reality. I felt almost "brain dead" as I went through this horrible experience. It helped me to make some decisions and not let others decide everything for me.

Avoid the temptation to escape through tranquilizers and alcohol. This can be tempting, but only compounds your problems. I made a decision to avoid that temptation.

I'M MAKING IT . . . DAY BY DAY

My struggle is far from over. But I've learned that I'm stronger than I thought. Oh, I'm not real strong, but I am making it. I've been subpoenaed to testify before a judge about Chuck's death. I am a witness since I found him the day he died. There will be the sentencing of the murderer. I know all this will cause me to relive the horror. I've made it through the first year and I know I can make it from here on with the help of God, my daughter, my family, and my friends.

I'm looking to the future. I have thought a lot about how I might use my experience to help others. I'm hoping to organize a support group for victims of violence—those who are suffering through the tremendous emotional upheaval and difficult adjustment to loss from violent death. It's not just the loss of one you love, but also the incredible pain of being a suspect in the crime yourself. In addition, there are many days in court that drag on and on. The legal process has kept the pain stirred up in my own life, and has forced me to replay the horrible scenes in my mind—in living color. It was a great relief when Chuck's murderer was sentenced to life in prison with no parole. It helps me to know he won't be able to hurt another family.

Don't be surprised if family and friends don't talk about the death. Many people said, "Call me anytime you need to," but rarely did anyone call me. I became upset because I didn't hear from them. I finally called some friends. But it was very hard for me to call anyone. If you really want to be a friend to people who are grieving, don't say, "Call me." Call them.

I want to learn from my experiences and help others going through the horror. I want to be able to tell them in person, "I'm making it—and so can you!"

FOOTPRINTS

One night I dreamed a dream.
I was walking along the beach with my Lord.
Across the dark sky flashed scenes from my life.
For each scene, I noticed two sets
Of footprints in the sand,
One belonging to me
And one to my Lord.
When the last scene of my life shot before me,
I looked back at the footprints in the sand.
There was only one set of footprints.
I realized that this was at the lowest
And saddest times in my life.
This always bothered me
And I questioned the Lord
About my dilemma.
"Lord, you told me when I decided to follow you,
You would walk and talk with me all the way.
But I was aware that during the most troublesome
Times of my life, there is only one set of footprints.
I just don't understand why, when I needed you most,
You leave me."
He whispered, "My precious child,
I love you and I will never leave you.
Never, ever, during your trials and testings.
When you saw only one set of footprints,
It was then that I carried you."

—Margaret Fishback Powers

Rachael was twelve years old when she watched the dad she dearly loved slowly die from cancer.

Now, one year later, she offers wisdom gained through her experience that will help other teens cope with the loss of a parent—and help the surviving parent understand the feelings of a grieving teen.

10

Rachael's Story:
My Home Video of Dad

You are the helper of the fatherless.

Psalm 10:14

I made my bed on the tiny green couch in the living room so I could sleep near my dying father. We had a real close relationship. He was more than a father to me; he was a real good friend. Before he became ill we watched scary western movies together; he took me shopping, he took me to buy candy, and out to eat with him and Mom. At night when Mom would still be downstairs working, I would climb in bed with my dad and we would read together. He was kind and showed his love in many ways.

Dad started to have stomach pain that wouldn't go away. X-rays and tests showed that he had colon cancer. I was eleven years old and in the fifth grade then. Following surgery and chemotherapy he was well for several months and then the cancer came back. They operated again, but this time they were unable to remove all of it because it was wrapped around his aorta. He took radiation, but didn't want more chemotherapy as it made him very ill. He became weaker and we put a hospital bed in our living room. He was given intravenous fluids because he could not eat. A nurse came every day to take care of him.

"HE'S GONE."

My mom, my fourteen-year-old brother, Chris, and I, watched him slowly dying. That was worse than his actual death. It was confusing, nerve racking, and emotionally uncontrollable to watch helplessly as the dad we loved grew weaker. I tried to be happy for him. I smiled even though I had to fake it. I told him I loved him. I fed him ice chips. I turned the television on for him. I'd hug him often. I tried to keep him happy during the time he had left with us.

He told us he was going to die. "Take good care of your mother," he told me. "Don't fight with Chris, take care of yourself, and keep your grades up at school."

I could tell by looking at him that he was becoming much worse. Then I heard Mom on the phone with Grandma. She said, "You'd better come. He's real bad and I don't know how much longer he will be here."

I slept on the little green couch just to be near him that night.

The next morning, a friend of mine stopped by to walk me to school. I was twelve years old and in the sixth grade. I gave dad a hug and a kiss and said, "Good-bye, Dad, I love you." He was very weak and only partially conscious at times, but this morning he knew who I was. "I love you too, Rachael," he said.

I went on to school.

At the beginning of fifth hour, we were just leaving our classroom to go to the library. The teacher locked her door and then she heard the phone ringing. It was a message for me to meet my brother, Chris, in the office and then we were to go home. A terrible feeling came over me. Dad is dying, I thought. Or maybe he already died.

On the way to the office, while I was worrying about what I would find when I arrived home, I met this boy that I could never stand. He always said mean, sarcastic things to me. This time was no different. "Why do you have to go to the office, Rachael? Are you in trouble, or did somebody die or something?"

I felt so angry at him, I wanted to punch him. Why does he have to be mean to me now, when I am so worried about Dad?

Our pastor met us in the school office and drove us home. I threw my books right down in the front yard and ran into the house. I looked at my dad, and I couldn't tell if he was asleep or dead. Chris kept hugging and kissing Dad.

Then Mom said, "He's gone."

I went to Dad and just kept hugging him.

ANGER, GUILT, AND OTHER EMOTIONS

The hearse came to take my dad away. Grandma arrived as the hearse came. That was best because Dad did not want his mother to see him die.

Chris and Mom went to the funeral home to pick out a casket. Then Mom and I went to the cemetery to choose the burial spot and the grave stone. We spent the next two evenings at the funeral home where we cried and cried. Many friends came to the funeral and most of them were young people. The ground was too hard and cold to dig a grave so we had a service at the mausoleum and we cried some more.

It has been one year and two months since my dad died. My biggest problem is not having him here. I miss having him to talk to, to help me with my homework, to go to my dance recitals, to watch movies with me. I am so lonely at times that I feel absolutely lost. I can't find my way.

There were times I felt that there was no use going on. I wanted to just sit and wait for God to come and get me. I thought to myself, I might as well sit in the corner and eat worms!

It has helped to meet other teens who have lost a parent or other family member. I met them at a center called Eli's Place, where grieving children, teens, and adults share their feelings. I go there once a week and will continue to go until I feel I can be strong and know that I'm beyond my grief.

There are so many feelings you go through when someone close to you dies. One of those feelings is anger. I was mad at God. It seemed He was to blame for my dad's death. I felt very frustrated and aggravated. My dad's death was so unfair! I am getting over it now. I realize I can't really be mad at God when I ask myself, "Would I rather have Dad here suffering or have him in heaven, where he's not hurting at all?" When I think about it that way, I can't be mad at God for taking Dad out of his suffering.

Another emotion I've had a hard time with is guilt. There were many things I wanted to say to Dad before he died. I knew what I was going to say, but I didn't want to tell him when he couldn't hear me. He'd listen in his weak, semiconscious state, but he wouldn't actually hear me. I wanted him to know and understand what I was saying. I know he knew I loved him, but I didn't get a chance to say, "I'm sorry for some of the things I've done." Or to say, "Thank you for putting up with my brattyness, for being there for me to talk to, for being a real father, instead of just someone who doesn't care."

I kept the guilt inside for all those things I could have said but never did, and then—and this is really wrong—I took my guilt out on my mom and my brother. Guilt is being angry at yourself. When you push that anger off on to someone else, it just makes everybody miserable.

There were times I wasn't myself. I lost control and didn't know what I was doing. Sometimes I didn't even know the reason I was so angry. I yelled at my mom. I talked back. Once I was so mad at myself about something I hadn't said to Dad, I got upset and aggravated at my mom and she slapped me. Then I hit her back. I really regret that. I was so angry I didn't know what I was doing. I was acting foolish and childish. It seemed she wouldn't talk to me. She wouldn't listen or try to understand me.

The way it worked in our family was like this: I talked to Dad, Mom talked to Dad, Chris talked to Mom. After Dad died it seemed I didn't have anyone to talk to. I kept asking, "Who am I going to talk to?"

Then Mom started talking to her high school sweetheart that she knew before she met my dad. I was jealous and envious and didn't know how to handle the situation.

But despite these problems, of all the people who have helped me, my mom has helped me the most. My friends and my pastor have helped, and the people at Eli's Place. Since I've been going there, I've really had a change of attitude. I learned to face what I felt; not to keep feelings bottled up; to let people know what I am feeling. If we don't get our feelings out in the open, they just get worse and worse, and more and more bitter, until we can hardly function anymore.

People brought in meals for us and phoned, and that was helpful. But my very best friend didn't know what to say. She was the one person I thought would be there for me more than anyone else in the whole world, but she wasn't. My dad was like a dad to her too. Friends I thought would be there disappeared and those I didn't expect were there!

THE SURVIVING PARENT'S ROLE IN A CHILD'S RECOVERY

My mom went with me to Eli's Place, and there I was able to share what I was feeling with other people who understood me. At that point, Mom had worked through a lot of her grief and she didn't have as many problems dealing with her grief as I did with mine. She just had this hurt in her memory. But she knew I needed help so she went with me. She had to dig up all that anger and the other emotions again and talk about it. It has been really hard for her. She loved me enough to go through all that pain in order to help me through my grief. I admire her for that.

Even before we started going to Eli's Place, Mom talked to me and let me express my feelings in my own way, understanding that I wasn't taking it out on her personally. It helped a lot. If I blew up in her face she would help by saying softly, "Calm down, go read or go do something else."

Parents can become so caught up in their own feelings that they think the kids have everything covered. It's a mistake to think that. Kids have problems too. Parents know it, but sometimes they don't really understand. They need to ask themselves, "What would it be like if I were a teenager and my dad or mom died?" Parents should ask their teens questions such as: "Is there something you want to talk about? Are you having problems? Is everything okay?" Be sure to tell them, "When you are having problems you can talk to me."

If the teen doesn't want to be in the place where the person died, don't make them go there. Our dad died in our living room and it was very hard for Chris to go in there. So we took up the carpet, bought new furniture and painted the walls a different color. Those changes made it easier for Chris to go in that room again.

Friends and other folks need to ask, "Do you feel comfortable talking about your parent's death?" Give teens permission to talk, but don't force them to talk because it may make them sad or depressed. They may not be ready yet. When they're ready, if you tell them you want to listen, then they will talk.

When people would ask me how I was doing, I didn't want to be rude, so I would grit my teeth and say, "I'm fine." I realize now that it is best not to become angry, but to say instead, "I am not comfortable discussing it yet."

MY HOME VIDEO: RACHAEL AND DAD

For other teens who have lost a parent my advice is, deal with it. Don't bottle up your feelings.

I never thought of suicide, but I know some people do when they get really depressed. Anyone who gets that depressed should be sure to talk to someone right away. If you feel like you don't want to live, then trust me when I say this: You will get better, you will feel better. Don't do anything to yourself that you can't undo. Sure, it'll be real hard to keep going on, but grief isn't forever. Life does get better if you stick with it.

You can't spend your life moping around. Be happy! You probably think, "Be happy? How can I be happy after losing someone I love?"

Here's how: When you think of the person who died, think of the good times—not the bad ones. Think of what he or she would want you to do: Would that person want you to be sad or happy? Don't sit around feeling sorry for yourself. Get on with your life. If a flower, picture, or song makes you think of that person, then fine, think happy thoughts. Don't allow it to get you down.

When people die, they're gone. You can't change that. But you can dedicate the things you do to their memory. I love ballet and jazz dancing. My dad used to come to my recitals. When I dance I try to think, Hey, Dad, this one is for you! I think of my dad when I hear the song "Rock of Ages" because he sang it just before he died. When I hear that song I think about him being happy in heaven. When I sing in the church choir, I think of how proud my dad is of me.

I wish my dad could be here for my graduation, my wedding, for the birth of any children I may have. It's hard to see my mom with another man. If she decides to get married again it's her decision and I will support her, even though I don't particularly like the idea. But if she is happy, I will be happy for her. We have to handle these situations the best we can.

If we still have one parent we are lucky. A lot of kids have no parent at all. The worst thing to do is to take out your anger and grief on the parent who is left. Don't do that! Because if something happens to that parent, you will not only have to work through the grief of losing that person, but also the guilt from having hurt that person.

Find something you can cherish, something that reminds you of the person who has died. Maybe it's something he or she gave you, something that person said to you, maybe a picture, a letter, or a piece of jewelry. Write it down, take it out, look at it, hold it, read it over and over.

Almost everything I have reminds me of my dad. I'll be alone and I'll take out a memory and look at it. It's just for me to see; no one else can see my memory. It can be a special shared moment, stored away in my thoughts.

Keep remembering happy thoughts of your loved one. Never forget that person. Replay the happy times again and again, like a favorite video, like a movie that you run through your mind, little pictures running smoothly along—and you don't have to see anything you don't want to see. You can also use your imagination and put little extra things into the pictures to make it fun and exciting. I think of it as my home video, Rachael and Dad.

Some people may say things to you that seem rude, mean, and obnoxious. Don't allow what others say to get you down. It hurts when people ask, "Where does your dad work?" or when someone on the phone says, "May I speak to your dad?" But they don't know any better. Try to let it pass.

If my story is published it may help someone and that is something I can be proud of. I might even prevent a teen from considering suicide. My dad used to tell us, "God works in mysterious ways." I hope God can use my experience to help another teen.

....

ROCK OF AGES

Rock of Ages, cleft for me,
Let me hide myself in Thee;
Let the water and the blood,
From Thy wounded side which flowed,
Be of sin the double cure,
Save from wrath and make me pure.

Could my tears forever flow,
Could my zeal no languor know,
These for sin could not atone
Thou must save, and Thou alone
In my hand no price I bring,
Simply to Thy cross I cling.

While I draw this fleeting breath,
When my eyes shall close in death,
When I rise to worlds unknown
And behold Thee on Thy throne,
Rock of Ages cleft for me,
Let me hide myself in Thee

—Augustus M. Toplady

How can a wife possibly cope when the love of her life is snatched from her without warning and she has four children to raise?

Sharon's biggest struggle was single parenting. She shares important lessons God is teaching her and offers suggestions for others.

11

Sharon's Story:
FATHER TO THE FATHERLESS

Yet I am always with you;
you hold me by my right hand.
You guide me with your counsel,
and afterward you will take me into glory.
Whom have I in heaven but you?
And being with you,
I desire nothing on earth.
My flesh and my heart may fail,
but God is the strength of my heart
and my portion forever.

Psalm 73:23-26

My husband, Keith, loved to fly. He learned to fly at an early age with his father, who owned a small private plane. Later he flew fighter planes in the Air Force and then flew with the National Guard. Eventually he owned his own small plane and it was pure joy for him to go flying as often as he could.

He also loved the Lord Jesus and had a deep concern for others. He made time in his busy schedule for the church and for people who needed help. It was natural for him to be excited at the prospect of flying Dr. and Mrs. Cropsey—who were missionaries to Africa—to meetings in another state. I flew along with Keith and the Cropseys. We returned the next day, landing on the sod strip at our farm. After we unloaded, Dr. Cropsey and his wife left for home.

Keith was planning to fly Dr. Cropsey to another meeting the next day, but first he needed to refuel at a small airport nearby. He suggested that Timothy and I go along. "You could hold Timothy so he won't be scared of the banking turn before we land," he said.

"Okay," I replied. I picked up Timothy and started to climb into the plane. Then I stepped back out and said, "No, I'd better not go." I had been feeling queasy on our return flight and didn't want to become ill and frighten Timothy any more than he already was.

Keith gave us each a hug, waved good-bye and flew off. I left to pick up our children from school: Kristin, age 17; Jay, 14; and Matthew, 11. When we returned home Keith wasn't back yet. I had an uneasy feeling. But Jay had an appointment to see a doctor at the hospital, so we had to leave again right away. When we returned from the hospital, I still didn't see the plane. I felt panic rising.

Approaching the house, I noticed a car in our driveway that I didn't recognize. Now I was really in a panic. I rationalized that since it wasn't a police car, things must be all right. When I walked through the door, two police officers were standing in our kitchen. That's when I felt overwhelmed by the reality that something terrible had happened. I felt my knees wobbling. I leaned against the sofa to keep from falling.

"Is he alive?" I asked. "That's all I need to know."

"Yes," one of the officers replied. "He's alive, and I'll drive you to the hospital."

CLINGING TO HOPE

Keith had left the airport to come home. As he cleared the trees at the end of the runway, a shaft in the fuel injector broke and the engine died. He managed to land in a newly planted field, but the impact tore off the front landing gear and ripped off most of one wing. Keith took the full impact with his head.

As we drove to the hospital, I thought, I can hardly breathe! I should be making conversation, but I can't think of anything to say. I realized that Jay and I had been at the hospital for his appointment ninety minutes earlier when, unknown to us, the medical helicopter had landed there with Keith.

My sense of dread and panic was so strong as I approached the hospital door, I felt like bolting in the opposite direction. I forced myself to calm down and go in, and as soon as I passed through the door of the hospital, I saw several familiar faces, all friends from our church. I was grateful that they had dropped what they were doing to come be with Keith and me.

The nurse directed me to the family waiting room. My children were being brought to the hospital by other family members, and they had not arrived yet. I didn't want to go into that empty waiting room alone, but as I looked inside, I realized the room was not empty. My pastor was there. God knew how desperately I needed Christian love and support, and He had it waiting for me through my pastor and church friends.

In a few minutes the doctor entered, very brisk and business-like. "Your husband has a severe closed head injury," he said. "It does not look good, not even hopeful."

I felt suddenly very angry at the doctor as I listened to his pessimistic pronouncement.

Our friend, Dr. Cropsey, was on duty and I felt comforted having him there. "If Keith makes it through the night," he said reassuringly, "it will be encouraging. God is in the miracle performing business." I kept clinging to that hope.

Dr. Cropsey found beds for us so we could lie down and get some rest. I kept getting up and talking to Keith. I was ecstatic that Keith made it through the night even though he was on life support.

The doctor repaired the damage to Keith's ankle. They must think he is going to make it, I thought. But later that day, two EEGs showed no brain activity. We had to face the horrible reality that we were losing him.

The nurse on duty was professional, but seemed cold and uncaring. Didn't any of these people understand what a wonderful person Keith is? It made me angry to see my husband treated as a set of vital signs attached to a respirator rather than as a loving, caring human being.

Finally, the doctors made it clear that there was no hope for Keith. A nurse asked us to sign a consent form to donate Keith's organs and keep him alive on life support for five or six hours until they could remove them. I was horrified. I don't want him touched, I thought. Why are you so demanding? Where is your compassion? It was as if Keith were being reduced to some non-human state. It was an agonizing decision, but the children and I knew that even in death Keith would want to help others. Consequently, we signed the papers for removal of his organs.

My feet felt like lead as I walked out of the hospital that evening. **He is still alive,** I thought. **Why am I leaving?**

But he is was not really alive.

Cars were driving past, people were walking here and there. I wondered, How can they go on as if nothing has happened? Keith has left this world, my whole world has just been shattered, yet life just goes on for everyone else. I was furious with the doctor, the nurse who asked for Keith's organs, and an entire world which refused to stop and notice my pain. My children were hungry. **What will I feed them? How can I even think of preparing food?**

As we entered our house, we found a beautiful deli tray on the table. God, through His people, was already providing for our needs.

WHAT IS MY ROLE NOW?

For me, Keith was everything: my best friend, my love, my problem solver, my exhorter, and sometimes my father. Life without him seemed absolutely impossible at first. I had so many fears. How could I ever make big decisions without his wisdom, experience, and common sense? How could I face illness and growing old without him? I ached with the fear of going places without his strength and presence with me. But the greatest fear of all was facing the enormous task of raising our children alone.

I knew the Bible teaches that God is Father to the fatherless, but I still felt an enormous pressure to become both mom and dad. I was wading into uncharted waters—and I was overwhelmed. Should I try to be a comedian like Keith was? Was it now my job to take the boys fishing, hiking, and camping? Was it now my job to expose them to the values of manhood that Keith had been planning to instill in them? What was my role, now that Keith was gone? Keith had always been the strong authority figure in our home, not me—and I didn't want the job!

Like it or not, however, I was now the authority figure to three boys and a daughter. I felt completely lacking in confidence, wisdom, and common sense. I realized now that I was the only example in the home, and that they were watching me. I didn't want to become a loud, pushy, hollering authority (that wasn't Keith's style, anyway). I must work at being a godly, feminine example. I kept praying that God would give me wisdom to be the consistent, disciplined person I knew I needed to be. My husband was the good example of this. He also gave me a great gift by establishing respect and honor for me in our home. The children were taught to obey and not talk back. That didn't eliminate problems with them, but it could have been much more painful for me if he had not established a disciplined respectful environment.

I spent much of that first year on my knees. Of course that's exactly where I needed to be. At times it seemed almost unbearable. The children and I were each dealing with this horrible loss in our own way.

Kristin felt a lot of anger and bitterness at God. Her dad missed her graduation. She was looking forward to learning from her dad how to fly that summer. The Christian college Keith and I and Kristin had decided on was ten hours away. She dreaded the homesickness, but her dad had promised that he would fly out for her on special weekends. Kristin and I began to argue about every small decision and then came the big issue of her leaving for college. She decided she did not want to go. But I knew that it was best for her spiritual growth to be in that Christian environment.

This was a supreme test of my authority and my boys needed to see that I wouldn't back down on an issue I felt was crucial to Kristin's spiritual life. Now, two years later, we can all look back and agree that the decision was best. God brought people at that college into Kristin's life who helped her realize there truly was anger and bitterness in her life that had to be dealt with. She also realizes that the reason I wanted her to go away to school was because I truly wanted the best for her, not because I didn't love her.

After Kristin left for college there were only four around the table at mealtime. Keith was a teaser and joker. He usually had us laughing about something. Kristen was bubbly and talkative much like her dad. Now I could barely endure sitting through a quiet, uneventful, boring meal without the glaring losses washing over me again and again. As a result we went to a lot of drive-through windows at fast-food places.

After a while, I realized that our fast-food diet was affecting our physical and mental health. I was in charge now and must do what was best for my family. It was a decision of the will: I would begin taking an interest in cooking again. We worked at solving the quiet table by getting to know each other better. We bathed our family times in prayer, and claimed God's promise to supply grace, wisdom, and strength. I continually reminded myself that God is Father to my children and loves them even more than I do.

Jay, a sophomore, had spent much time with his dad, repairing machinery and tearing motorcycles apart. He became my fix-it man. He also underwent a lot of spiritual growth in the wake of his father's death, and has become more outgoing than before. Jay just completed twelve hours of flight instruction which I've had to turn totally over to the Lord.

Matthew is an eighth grader in junior high school now. Of all the kids, he seemed to withdraw the most. It is difficult to know how much of his behavior is due to his dad's death and how much is normal for his age. I continue to pray for him intensely as I do for all my children.

Timothy, our little guy, has already forgotten so much about his dad that it saddens me. We all try to talk about Keith and the things he did to keep his memory alive.The loss of intimacy is difficult for me because it involved so many levels of relationship. I miss discussing a problem and holding Keith's hand in church. Sleeping on his side of the bed, wearing his pajamas, keeping pictures close by, all seem to help me feel closer to him. Some days I only think of him occasionally and other days I miss him all day. Small things—for example, seeing one of the boys walking across the yard wearing his jacket—can send huge waves of sadness and loneliness washing over me.

GETTING ON WITH MY LIFE

It has been a healing balm for me to step back into the church organ ministry. It is the only area of my life that hasn't changed. When I play I feel enclosed in a safe, peaceful cocoon and I can retreat into the past as long as I don't look out into the congregation and see an empty seat where Keith used to be. I remember when God called me into this ministry; I didn't want to do it. I didn't feel talented enough. But because of the need for an organist, and with Keith's encouragement, I finally surrendered. God knew I'd need one area in my life that remained constant. This visible ministry has also given me an opportunity to demonstrate to my children that my faithfulness to God's work and calling doesn't depend on circumstances.

Two years after Keith's death, all our children and I shared in an experience that was very healing. We traveled with my father-in-law and sixteen people from our church to Togo, West Africa, to build a Bible institute to train some Togolese people to pastor their own churches. Keith's memorial money went toward one of those buildings. I agonized terribly over the decision to go. I didn't know if I could stand the pain associated with memories of Keith. I wasn't convinced that it was a wise way to spend a large sum of money. I felt an overpowering fear of flying, especially across the ocean.

Finally I prayed, "Lord, I don't know the best thing to do. I will make plans to go and if it is not the right decision, put an obstacle in my way." No obstacles presented themselves, so we went. That trip was a turning point for all of us as we saw something very good resulting from something so horrible.

After we returned from Togo, I became very ill from a reaction to the malaria medicine and for the first time since Keith's death I was forced to be in bed many days. It gave me lots of time to reflect and evaluate the past two years. I realized that I had substituted being busy for grieving. I had filled my days with ceaseless activity and my nights with reading. That was my version of coping. But I wasn't so much coping as I was avoiding having to cope. I was so busy, I didn't have time to be a mom. I was too busy to take adequate care of our home, to cook decent meals, or to help our family fully process our loss.

The trip to Togo helped me to finally face Keith's death. The final chapter of our lives together had been written and I must look to the future. I realized how much my children meant to me. I felt guilty for the many mistakes I had made since Keith's death and I told God if He would help me through this time of illness, I would get my priorities straight.

I decided I needed the help of a Christian support group. At the time I had an overwhelming fear that someone there would think I was looking for a "replacement" for Keith. But I had to overcome that hesitation and do what was right for my own recovery. I also realized that the children needed a support system as well. I wasn't able to help them with their grief because I was barely surviving my own grief and my new responsibilities.

God has helped me realize that my first responsibility is to maintain a close relationship with Him through prayer, Bible study, and fellowship with other Christians. Second, I must be a godly mom. Third, I must be a part of advancing His kingdom by serving Him faithfully in whatever place He calls me.

I'm daily seeking God's strength and trying, often unsuccessfully, to live one day at a time without worrying about tomorrow. I'm often frustrated because I focus too much on what I want to accomplish and not enough on the progress I'm making. But God is helping me and healing me of my tendency to blame and condemn myself, and the load of guilt is lessening. Psalm 139:7-10 has become very precious to me:

> Where can I go from your Spirit?
> Where can I flee from your presence?
> If I go up to the heavens, you are there;
> if I make my bed in the depths, you are there.
> If I rise on the wings of the dawn,
> if I settle on the far side of the sea,
> even there your hand will guide me,
> your right hand will hold me fast.

God is always with me. His right hand is always there waiting for me to take it. He will guide and direct me. What a comforting thought!

My relationship with God is now a daily reality. I am often in desperate need of His wisdom and help to overcome fears, to deal with parenting problems, and to be the godly, consistent, disciplined mother I want to be. My prayer life has gone from one of generalities and quick, tired prayer at the end of the day to earnest specific prayer.

HOW TO BE A FRIEND TO A GRIEVING SINGLE PARENT

Our church family, our pastor, the Christian school, our family, and friends have been wonderful. The intercessory prayer, hugs, words of encouragement, cards, breakfast invitations, and books have all helped. Reading helped me realize that others have gone through experiences like mine, survived—and even grown. I can already look back and see much growth for our entire family, but it hasn't come easily. Caring people have helped in many ways.

It is difficult to go places alone. Recently a friend invited me to a Bible study for women who have been through loss. I know I wouldn't have attended, even though I wanted to, unless my friend had taken me.

At times food holds little appeal and it is easy to make excuses for not cooking—even though I don't want to jeopardize my family's health by not providing nutritious meals. A big pot of soup in a throw-away container or an occasional meal provided by a friend can give a single parent an uplift—and a break.

It frightens me to think of attempting to drive my boys to another city to see a professional basketball game. It is wonderful for other families to include bereaved children in outings like this. It's very encouraging to know your children are doing something they enjoy in a setting with a dad, and it gives the single mom a breather.

When two or three women go to a play or concert it is a wonderful gesture of love to invite a widowed, divorced, or single friend to go along. And don't be offended if she declines. It takes time to be able to go places and do things without feeling the intense pain of one's loss.

Don't try to take your friend's mind off her loss; don't hesitate to bring it up. The best therapy for me has been to just talk about Keith and my feelings. It is good to ask specific questions such as, "How are you sleeping—or are you?" These kinds of questions help open up the doors of communication. But whatever you do, don't say, "I know how you feel." (You probably don't.)

Avoid quoting Bible verses when the loss is fresh. When people did that with me, I knew those verses were meant as a help, but I couldn't make them a reality in my life at first. The pain was too great. And when you feel like people are prodding you to be spiritual when you simply don't have the strength and perspective to be spiritual, it can add to your pain by making you feel guilty—or angry.

Looking back, I can see the clarity of God's direction in putting Keith in the airplane by himself. I know that God has not made a mistake. What would have become of my children if both of their parents—and Timothy— had been killed by that crash?

For a long time I looked upon my reaction to loss and grief as a weakness in my faith. I still struggle with my feelings at times. I am learning not to feel like a failure as a Christian, just because I make mistakes or show human weakness. As I reflect on my life since Keith has been gone, I can recognize the many times God's strength has been made perfect through my weakness. My emphasis has to be not on how I am doing, but on how much I am allowing Him to work through me. I am learning that I am nothing without Him, but that I can do all things through Christ who strengthens me. It is a daily struggle, but He is patiently teaching me and I can see glimpses of the progress I'm making.

A favorite Scripture passage of mine is Psalm 143:8, "Let the morning bring me word of your unfailing love, for I have put my trust in you. Show me the way I should go, for to you I lift up my soul." One thing I can depend on in my changing world is the faithfulness of my loving heavenly Father.

....

THE WEAVER

Our lives are but fine weavings
That God and we prepare,
Each life becomes a fabric planned
And fashioned in His care.

We may not always see just how
The weavings intertwine,
But we must trust the Master's hand
And follow His design.

For He can view the pattern
    Upon the upper side,
While we must look from underneath
    And trust in Him to guide.

Sometimes a strand for sorrow
    Is added to His plan,
And though it's difficult for us
    We still must understand.

That it's He Who fills the shuttle,
    It's He Who knows what's best,
So we must weave in patience
    And leave for Him the rest.

Not till the loom is silent
    And the shuttles cease to fly
Shall God unroll the canvas
    And explain the reason why—

The dark threads are as needed
    In the Weaver's skillful hand
As the threads of gold and silver
    In the pattern He has planned.

                        —Author unknown

How should we react to a family member's gay lifestyle and the diagnosis of AIDS? Should we tell our family and friends? Should we hide the truth? What should our attitude be toward our loved one's gay partner?

In her own words, Gloria relates the story of her family's personal struggle with these questions. You will walk with Gloria and her family through the agonizing illness and death of her brother Gary—and you will learn about how to love someone, even when loving isn't easy.

12

Gloria's Story:
WHAT AIDS COULD NOT TAKE AWAY

Our Father in heaven,
hallowed be your name,
your kingdom come,
your will be done
on earth as it is in heaven.
Give us today our daily bread.
Forgive us our debts,
as we also have forgiven our debtors.
And lead us not into temptation,
but deliver us from the evil one.

Matthew 6:9–13

I grew up with three brothers. Gary was the oldest and he always seemed to have a special devotion to me, because I was his only sister. When he was twenty-seven years old, he told me he was gay.

I have never fully understood homosexuality. But, despite his sexual orientation, he was my brother and I loved him. Nevertheless, I had concerns about Gary's contact with my young sons and I felt relieved that we lived a great distance apart.

The next time I heard from Gary he was living in San Francisco. Mom bravely went there to visit him. She found him living in a posh apartment with four or five other gay men. She was making an honest effort to understand homosexuality and what was happening to her son. We had been brought up in the church, and Mom felt responsible and guilty because of Gary's lifestyle.

Following a year in San Francisco, Gary moved in with our grandmother for a while, and then went home to live with our parents. He became financially dependent on them. He was a high achiever in college, but he never found employment related to his degree. He was a flamboyant, interesting person with a love for the humanities. He worked at several art galleries and became a respected art and literature critic. Eventually he found a job with the Institute of Arts and moved into an apartment. Later he bought his own home.

Gary liked my husband, Jeff, and the three of us talked often on the phone. Because I'm a registered nurse, Gary would call for consultation with his health problems which seemed to be increasing.

A REASON TO HANG ON TO LIFE

In 1980 we knew very little about AIDS. I was also in denial and didn't recognize what was right in front of my eyes. Gary's immune system was depressed by the AIDS virus, leaving him susceptible to illness. I kept urging him to go to the doctor for tests. He finally followed my advice and I heard from my parents in July that Gary was HIV positive. Again, I was not really surprised, knowing about Gary's lifestyle, but I felt terribly sad and sorry for the brother I loved.

My caregiver instincts longed to find the best treatment for him, but I felt he must tell me himself that he was HIV positive before I could proceed. I began to feel totally frustrated and wrote him a letter saying I knew his diagnosis and wanted to help. I put off mailing the letter and waited for word from Gary. In October, three months after his family doctor confirmed that he had AIDS, Gary gave me the bad news.

He had a hard time believing his diagnosis, trusting his doctor, and complying with treatment. His doctor was competent, understanding, and kind, but he was learning about AIDS just like the rest of us. I started phoning, networking, and seeking the very best treatment I could find to help Gary. I had him signed up for an experimental treatment but he refused to go, despite his increasing health problems which included a couple bouts with pneumonia.

Then we learned that he had decided to stop taking his AZT (medicine for AIDS). He was losing his judgment, but it was hard to tell if the AIDS was affecting his brain, if his attitude was related to his personality, or if he had a mental disorder. I wished I could have forced him to comply with his treatment, but he was an independent thirty-eight-year-old adult. He had to take responsibility for his own choices.

Gary did not withdraw from our family, and we supported and loved him. When he joined us for our Thanksgiving celebration, he looked pale and thin. The next month, at the completion of our Christmas gift exchange, my husband, Jeff, made this announcement to our family: "We have one more gift for you. It really cries and it really wets." We had four boys, the youngest was thirteen, and we had not planned to have more family—but suddenly we had a baby on the way!

Gary's response was one of exultation. He jumped a foot off the floor with glee. He grabbed me and hugged me. He was absolutely thrilled. It was an affirmation of life for him. It seemed that my pregnancy was a reason for him to hang on to life. It was the happiest I've ever seen him.

LOSING TOUCH WITH REALITY

I kept wondering what special thing I could do for Gary. Then I had an idea. Gary had told me he wanted a dog. He had never owned one. I thought, This is something I can do. He will love it!

I found out that the cost of a registered black Labrador was $300. While I was mustering up my courage to spend that big sum of money for the dog, our son had an accident with his bike. The people who came to his rescue were giving away beautiful puppies. They were a mixture of black Lab and German short hair pointers. I selected a puppy which we named Ginger and phoned Gary. He said, "That sounds great!"

We drove two hundred miles to take Ginger to him. We were so excited! Our excitement faded as we realized our plan would not work. Gary lived downtown with a small unfenced yard. Having a dog in the house made him terribly nervous. He couldn't deal with it. In a moment of weakness we decided to keep Ginger. I was seven months pregnant, had four boys and now a puppy to train. But we grew to love Ginger and she has become a special part of our family.

In the months prior to the birth of our daughter, Stephanie, Gary wrote letters with long lists of name possibilities. Sometimes he included as many as forty names and many of them seemed bizarre. Then he started telling us he was going to start his own art gallery. He would write letters with big words followed by huge exclamation points. He would phone at odd hours to tell us what the name of his art gallery was going to be. Then he lost his job at the art institute and he was convinced it was because of his AIDS diagnosis. He had taken the business from losing money to making money. What reason could there be for losing his job other than AIDS? His job loss and the helpless feeling from his AIDS prognosis plunged him into deep depression that resulted in hospitalization.

Gary was looking forward to Stephanie's birth with great anticipation, but he was too ill to be released from the hospital when she was born. There was much fear and uncertainty about AIDS, but I knew how important this baby was to Gary, so I prayed I would not make a foolish mistake. Two weeks after our beautiful daughter was born I made one of the hardest decisions I had ever made. I took her to the hospital two hundred fifty miles away and put her into the arms of my brother who was dying of AIDS. Even though he was deeply depressed and filled with fear, he radiated pride and joy as he held Stephanie. Her birth was a miracle to him.

Four months later he sent us four Thanksgiving cards. He did not remember he had sent more than one. The next month he joined us for our last family Christmas celebration together. His health had deteriorated. Brain damage was taking a toll. He was on a tangent about a big New Year's party we were going to have. We are not a family of big parties. We planned to spend the evening quietly at home with our children, but he was coming for the party and nothing would stop him.

The weather was foggy and the roads were icy on New Year's Eve. We were worried about Gary's safety during his four hour trip. He arrived safely with his partner, Jim. It was extremely difficult to welcome Jim and make friends with him, but for Gary's sake we did. We found him to be a kind, gentle person. He was ten years younger than Gary and also HIV positive. His family completely rejected him. He became almost like a member of our family as we all struggled through Gary's illness.

Gary talked incessantly. He would tell bizarre stories about our family based on a little fact and then go off into delusion. He kept us up the entire night. I had a little baby to care for. I didn't know what to do with Gary. He would say, "AIDS has run its course. It is not in my body any more. I have never felt better in my life!"

I kept saying, "You think everything is all right, but all these people sitting here are telling you that everything is not okay. Please do us a favor, go to the doctor and get checked out."

We were able to talk to Jim alone. "You absolutely must get help for Gary," we told him.

Jim did take Gary to a psychiatrist who said Gary's problem was not caused from a physical disease, but instead, from a mental condition. He was admitted to a private psychiatric unit, but he refused to cooperate with the treatment. Though he was warned that he would be transferred to a state hospital if he refused to cooperate, Gary continued to resist his treatment. And he was transferred.

CLOSER AS A FAMILY

By the middle of January, I had a baby, a full-time job as a high school teacher, and it was final exam time. I learned that Gary wouldn't eat or get out of bed and that he had lost thirty pounds in three weeks. I felt that I needed to help my parents take care of him. I contacted a nurse at the state hospital. "I believe this is not mental, but a physical disease that is causing Gary's problem," she said. "I have a plan whereby we can have Gary seen by a doctor and transferred to a general hospital. Because Gary is so uncooperative he will have to be transferred in a police car and have guards with him."

Jeff and I flew to meet with Gary, my father, the psychiatrist, and the family doctor at the doctor's office. What happened next was the most traumatic thing that has ever happened to me in my life. I walked into the doctor's office and I saw a decrepit old man who had not been shaved for three weeks while at the state hospital. That decrepit old man was my brother.

I was immediately angered over the apparent neglect that Gary had been treated with, but then I thought, Who wants to shave someone who is uncooperative and HIV positive? Gary looked like someone who had been found in the gutter. If I had not known he was my brother, I never would have recognized him. The psychiatrist wore rubber gloves, even though he was only pushing Gary's wheelchair, not examining or even touching Gary in any way. That angered me so much I wanted to rip those gloves right off him. Did he think he was going to catch AIDS from my brother's skin or his breath?

The only thing Gary would say to me was that this was all my fault. I had done this to him. I had insisted that he go for treatment and he remembered that. I felt horrible and blamed myself too. A CAT scan showed that half of Gary's brain was gone, atrophied from AIDS. The family doctor was shocked and saddened to see how Gary's condition had deteriorated.

I stayed with Gary several days, and we admitted him to a general hospital. He kept saying his address over and over because he wanted to go home. He kept reminding me that I was the person who put him there and I could arrange his discharge. He was bedridden and unable to walk. I knew he was going to die and I felt I should carry out his last wish and arrange to take him home. I considered taking a leave of absence from my job and having my mom help with Stephanie while I cared for Gary; but I had a husband and four boys. They were my primary responsibility. I had to realize that the nurses were capable and I wasn't the only person in the world who could take care of Gary; so I came home and Jeff and I visited him almost every weekend.

My father never missed one day of being with Gary in the hospital those eight weeks before he died. He was the only one who could make Gary eat. Mom spent a lot of time at Gary's bedside also. Jim visited regularly.

Gary had attended a Catholic church. His priest, Father Michael, was a wonderful person. He stood by and lovingly supported our entire family during Gary's illness and death. I read the Bible to Gary, though his attention span was very short. One of the last things he was able to do before he died was recite the Lord's Prayer. Even though he couldn't carry on a conversation that made sense, he could recite that prayer perfectly. He stayed mad at me, yet wanted me there. Because I am a nurse he saw me as his medical consultant. I made sure he had the best treatment available. However, none of it stopped the progress of his disease.

Gary went blind. I had seriously considered bringing him home until that time. Then I thought, **He won't be able to see anything. Going home is not as important now. He is receiving good care and the hospital is the best place for him.** About a week later, Gary slipped into a coma from which he never recovered.

Gary's illness was a severe financial hardship on my parents. They were responsible for expenses because Gary had no money. My dad learned that he could buy a cemetery lot cheaper while Gary was alive than after he died. I went with Dad to select one. We paid for the lot twelve hours before Gary died. It is one of those things you never forget. I was thinking, **He's alive—but he's not really alive!**

I stayed with Gary constantly the last two days and nights. I wanted to be sure all our family would be there with him when he died. As his vital signs weakened, I summoned my family and Father Michael. They arrived in time to share his last hour and a half on earth. We all stood around Gary's bed and held hands as Father Michael led us in the Lord's Prayer, feeling closer as a family than we have ever felt before. We were still holding hands and praying together when Gary breathed his last faint, shallow breath.

Death, we later learned, was caused by a virus that infected his brain. AIDS weakened his immune system and he could not overcome the infection.

The hospital personnel were wonderful. After Gary died, the person my parents wanted to thank the most was a student nurse. They sent a letter to her school, commending her. She seemed able to communicate well with Gary and she spoke about specializing in work with AIDS patients. I was so impressed by the way she and other nurses gave care without allowing any biases or moral judgments to get in the way.

ANGEL OF MERCY

The grief I felt was deep, and it lasted a long time. I didn't feel angry at God. Instead, my spiritual horizons were broadened as I learned and grew through my contact with Father Michael. I have had a lot of guilt to deal with over the fact that I never took Gary home. But every time I think it through, I come to the same conclusion: We did the best we could with what we knew at the time. AIDS is a mystery, even to the medical profession.

Some of the memories I have surrounding Gary's death are beautiful, such as the memory of our family joining hands and praying around his deathbed. But some of the memories are painful, and can still stir up anger within me. For example, the night before he died, they were still giving Gary breathing treatments. The therapist was yelling at Gary to take deep breaths, even though he was in a deep coma and not responding. I wondered, What is this accomplishing? I felt very angry and wanted to send her out of the room.

The doctor, hospital personnel, and our family were all learning about AIDS together. We felt helpless at times, but everyone did his or her best. I wore myself out physically and emotionally during Gary's illness. I was the mediator between my family and the medial profession interpreting information and relaying it back and forth. I was an advocate for Gary, trying desperately to see that he was given the best treatment available. After the funeral, we spent a week in Florida to get away and rest.

I was on my way to work the next week, preoccupied with thoughts of Gary's death. Intellectually I knew Gary was gone, but it still did not seem real. I was also dealing with the horrible guilt for not carrying out Gary's last wish to take him home. I turned on the radio and I heard the end of a song with the words, "She's all right, she's an angel," repeated over and over. Those words seemed to be coming directly from Gary to me. I felt somehow he was sending me a message that he had forgiven me for not taking him home and he was telling me I was an angel—an angel of mercy because of the many hours I cared for him in the hospital. I came unraveled, and had to pull off the road and regain my composure.

I went on to work at the school, still teary-eyed and shaky. Somehow I managed to make it through the day, although I felt overwhelmed by my responsibilities. The next morning I was completely exhausted, physically ill, and too weak to work. The doctor advised time off to rest and regain my health. Meanwhile the words of that song kept haunting me. I was determined to find it, but I didn't know the title or enough of the words to locate it. Finally I decided there wasn't really a song. It was truly a message from Gary to me.

During the next three years I did a lot of thinking and grieving. Recently I was sharing with one of my students whose father had died. I told her about the song. She was familiar with it. The next day she brought a tape with my "angel" song for my birthday. It was the perfect gift at just the appropriate time to give me closure in my grieving process.

Gary had a favorite song, "Have I Told You Lately (That I Love You)?" and he listened to that song repeatedly. It conveyed a message of love from him to our family who stood by him to the end. His other favorite was "Whenever God Shines His Light." Gary had confessed his sins and felt sure of heaven, so that song gave him hope as he looked forward to going there. As in the words of the song, God "opens up my eyes so I can see," Gary looked forward to being able to see again in heaven. Gary's blind eyes are open now and he can see the beauties of heaven.

That song also speaks of "the darkest night, deep confusion, great despair, and loneliness." During the horrible depression, mental confusion, and loneliness of AIDS, Gary was comforted by hearing, "When I reach out for Him, He is there, I know everything's going to be all right." The Christmas after he died I gave each of our family members a tape of these songs as a gift from Gary. I have kept my tape in my car and play those songs repeatedly. They have helped to heal my grief.

LESSONS FROM GARY'S LIFE

Over the past three years, as I've reflected on our experience with Gary, I've concluded that we learned several valuable lessons.

Our children learned something very important: No matter what you think, you still stand by. Be nonjudgmental, supportive, loving, and caring. They saw me stand by Gary and now they know that no matter what happens I will be there for them too.

A lesson I learned resulted from my failure to talk openly with Gary six months before his death. He was able to be out of the hospital and we were at our parent's home. He asked me, "What if I can't take care of myself?"

I replied, "We will always be there for you." That was the end of our conversation. That day I missed my chance to share his concerns and wishes. We never had another opportunity to really communicate effectively, so my advice to others in this situation is not to turn away from these opportunities. It is human nature to change the subject because it is painful to talk about death, but if I had known that Gary would be gone in six months, we would have had a long conversation.

It was three years before I could tell my students that my brother died of AIDS. It seemed too painful to talk about and I feared traumatizing the relationship between me and my high school students. Now I am becoming more aware that my role as a teacher gives me the opportunity to bring more understanding of AIDS—what the disease is and how best to deal with the victims and their families. AIDS is such a big issue for the students in my classes. They are struggling with tremendous pressure to be sexually active. They need to be fully informed about sexually transmitted diseases and realize that making the wrong choice can threaten their very lives.

Our family grew closer through this experience. We will always remember being united around Gary's bed and supporting him to the end. These are special times for families and it is important to be there together. Even if members are scattered and busy, it is important to put aside the busyness and unite. Issues and conflicts also need to be put aside at times of death. Crises can be turned into times of growth, healing, and strengthening of family ties.

Many people profited from this experience with Gary, but my mom learned and grew the most. It was very painful for her in several ways. Gary's departure from our Protestant upbringing was extremely difficult for her to accept. She worried greatly about Gary's eternal destiny. It made me angry when she initially would not accept Gary's Catholicism, but Father Michael allayed much of her concern. He was a wonderful person who provided Gary and all of us with spiritual comfort. He modeled unconditional love and acceptance. Father Michael preached Gary's funeral sermon, and about half of the people in attendance were from my mom's Protestant church. It was refreshing to see people of different religious persuasions coming together with hearts full of love and compassion. I wished Gary could have seen that.

My mom's church congregation stood by my parents, showing them tremendous love and support. They provided a delicious dinner for all of us after the funeral.

In addition to the religious issue, my mom had a hard time dealing with the stigma attached to AIDS. When her concerned co-workers kept asking about Gary, she replied, "We don't know what is wrong yet, they are still running tests." She felt unable to admit that Gary had AIDS. Maintaining this wall of secrecy caused a great deal of stress for her.

Everyone was supportive of our family, and Mom could have avoided much distress by sharing the truth with her friends, neighbors, and co-workers. My parents did become involved with a support group and that was a great help. There are still people who think AIDS could never affect them, but we know it has the potential of touching everyone. As the disease becomes more widespread, I believe attitudes will change and there will be less prejudice.

Our family now has a greater sensitivity and concern for AIDS victims and their families, more acceptance and love for those of different religious persuasions, and a greater appreciation of God's plan for our lives. These changes are reflected in a letter my mom wrote me three weeks after Gary's death. She related how friends that attend the Catholic church where Gary went had called to tell her about their Easter Sunday service. Father Michael had given a message on the theme, "Jesus Is Risen."

He told about visiting a terminally ill young man at the hospital many times in the past three months. He was talking about Gary, though he didn't use Gary's name. He told about becoming a friend to the young man's family, and that he was asked to come to the hospital the night Gary was dying. He was holding Gary's hand with the entire family around his bed. Little baby Stephanie was next to him in her mother's arms. She reached up to Gary and gently stroked his face. At that moment, this thought came to Father Michael: God takes life back to Himself, and He gives life. This little one will give the family something to hold on to and love, even while Gary is being missed. God surely helped bring healing and recovery to this family by sending them this little one.

"That's really true," Mom reflected when she heard about Father Michael's message. "I wish I could have been in that Easter service to hear Father Michael's message—though I'm sure I would have cried all the way through it. Father Michael was right. Gary was never happier than he was when he heard about Stephanie's arrival."

Mom called Jim, Gary's friend, and told him about Father Michael's sermon. Jim was pleased to hear that Father Michael had told Gary's story in the sermon. "That's really beautiful," he said. "Gary would be pleased to know that Father Michael was able to reach people's hearts through his story."

AIDS took my brother's life. But AIDS cannot take away love. We can choose to love, even in the midst of one of the most horrible and stigmatizing diseases ever known. I'm grateful to God that our family made the choice to draw close together in love, and I'm grateful that Gary is safe in the arms of our loving Father. My prayer is that many more hearts will be reached, touched, and healed through reading Gary's story in these pages.

....

HEALED AT LAST

In great confusion
    And deep despair,
I reach out to God,
    I know He is there.

When I am lonely
    As I can be,
I think of His love,
    That He is with me.

With blind eyes I live
    In the darkest night,
In heaven He'll open,
    And give me sight.

My strength He'll restore,
    All fear will be gone,
Only peace and joy,
    When heaven's begun.

—Ruth M. Sissom

Marge's experience proves that God can use anyone, anywhere, at any age. When we yield our lives completely to Him, He often surprises us with what He accomplishes through us.

13

Marge's Story:
Waitress, May We Have Our Check Please!

And we know that in all things
God works for the good of those who love him,
who have been called according to his purpose.

Romans 8:28

"Please provide a job for me, Lord," I prayed.

I had prayed that prayer for over a year and was beginning to wonder if it would ever be answered. It had been many years since I had worked outside my home and then only for a very short time. We had six children and my time had been occupied with caring for them. I loved to decorate cakes and for thirty-five years I had earned extra money creating special cakes for all kinds of occasions and selling them from my home. Our children were grown, and I was enjoying my home and my cake decorating business.

Then, without warning, my situation drastically changed.

My husband had a stroke and had to be admitted to a nursing home where—as it turned out—he would stay for ten and a half years. I had been relying on income from an investment. Then I was devastated by the loss of my invested money. All of our savings were gone, and the bills were exceeding my income.

As a result of the financial loss, the stress, and the loneliness I felt, I became extremely depressed. My children didn't want to be around me because I was "down" all the time. I decided I had to get out with other people to counteract the loneliness, and I had to earn some money to pay the bills. I had to find a job, but though I prayed earnestly and answered every ad in the newspaper, nobody would hire me. I began to despair of ever finding a job.

Then I saw an ad for waitress positions at a restaurant that was opening. I called the owner and asked for a job. He said, "Do you have young children?"

I burst out laughing. "I'm seventy-three years old!" I said.

I got the job!

To me it was a miracle of God that anyone would hire a seventy-three-year-old woman with no job history for the demanding job of waitress. But then, God is in the miracle business, isn't He?

WAITING TABLES, SERVING GOD

During that long, dreary, frustrating year while I had prayed for a job, I had also pleaded with God to use me in some way to do His work. There didn't seem to be anything I could do to really impact other lives for Him. Then one day God gave me an idea. I could write Christian messages on the back of my customer's meal checks. I began sharing my Scriptures as soon as I started working.

My biggest frustration with my new job was learning to work in harmony with others. The younger women complained that their feet hurt or about other aches and pains. But I felt great! It was a miracle from God that my feet and legs did not ache. I loved my job and the people I met each day. I have learned to pray that God will help me to concentrate on doing the best I can do each day; that I will be a good witness, bringing honor and glory to Him; and that I will be content to let Him shine through me.

I visited my husband at the nursing home every day. Occasionally, when the weather was nice, I would take him in his wheelchair across the street to a restaurant for an outing. I had to cross the railroad tracks and the wheels of the chair would get stuck in the grooves of the track. Many times after I managed to get him to the restaurant, my husband wouldn't eat. His mind had been affected by the stroke and he was never cheerful after that. As I look back, however, I can laugh about the frustration I felt as I struggled and struggled with that wheelchair, just so my husband could sit in that restaurant and refuse to eat!

As my husband's health deteriorated he was transferred from the nursing home to the hospital and back again several times. One Friday morning as I was preparing for work, my ailing husband was on my mind. He was in the hospital again, very ill with pneumonia. I suddenly felt a strong urge to go to the hospital and visit him. I prayed, "Lord, you know I have to go to work today, why do I have this feeling I should go see my husband? I'll be seeing him Sunday. Help me to know what I should do."

Just then, a friend called. I told her my dilemma, and she said, "I'll go with you. We can make it back in time for you to go to work."

I prayed, "Okay, Lord, if you want me to go see him I'll do it."

My friend and I traveled the thirty miles to the hospital. I told my husband I loved him and kissed him good-bye, never dreaming that would be the last time I would see him alive.

The next afternoon, my son called. "The hospital phoned," he said. "Dad is getting worse."

"I want to go see him," I replied.

It was the busy dinner hour at the restaurant, but I left and went to the nursing home with my son. When we arrived, my husband had already died.

GOOD FOR THE SOUL, GOOD FOR BUSINESS

God had been preparing me for this time through His Word. During the previous two years, I had spent each morning in the Bible, reading and praying, "Lord, lead me to the Scriptures I should write on my customer's checks today. You know each person I will meet. Give me just the right thoughts from Your Word that will give comfort and strength—whatever will minister to each person's need." Then I would write down the Scriptures and take them to work with me.

Most people who came to the restaurant would not understand many of the references I wanted to share with them, so I asked God for wisdom and put the verses in my own words to help make them clear, especially to folks who were not Bible readers. As I searched through the Bible for Scripture verses and wrote them down, God comforted and strengthened me through His Word.

One day a lady customer said to me, "I'm very ill from taking treatments for cancer. I feel really poorly today. I was feeling as if no one cared. Then I saw that you wrote on my check, JESUS CARES. Those words really encouraged me."

Another day I wrote on the back of a man's check, DO YOUR BEST AND GOD WILL DO THE REST. Sometime later, that man came back to the restaurant and said to me, "I had been on drugs and was to start rehab that day. I was so frightened, and I wondered if I could possibly make it through the treatment. When I saw what you had written, it gave me confidence. I decided to give it my very best effort and depend on God to help me. Well, here I am and I am making it."

In the four years I've worked at the restaurant, I've only had two people object to messages I wrote. I've had people ask me to pray for them and I've been able to share Christ. Some of the other messages I have written are:

We can depend on the Lord. He is always there for us.

Put your trust in the Lord Who does all things well.

Sometimes the Lord allows trials to come into our lives
to prepare us for greater things.

One day someone told me that a Sunday school teacher in a large church about thirty miles away had mentioned my ministry to his class. I was so surprised. Customers began requesting that I wait on them so they could receive my Scriptures. They would tell others and bring their friends with them to eat.

One day I said to my boss, "Do you know why your business is doing so well in spite of the recession?"

"Sure," he said. "It's our good prices."

"No, it isn't," I said. "God is blessing your business because you are allowing His Word to go forth from here. When I give customers their checks, it's not only good for the soul, it's good for business. Christian people are hearing about it and coming here to eat. And I want to thank you for allowing me to give out Scripture. I'm hoping you will become a Christian too."

I knew he would laugh at me, but I wanted to say it anyway.

Ruth Sissom recalls:

Recently my daughter and I had dinner at the Garden Patch restaurant where Marge works. I was amazed that at seventy-seven years of age, she still demonstrates such boundless energy. She was rushing around, taking orders, and satisfying all her customers' demands. She has a special twinkle in her eyes and a continuous smile. She is pleasant, friendly, and encouraging to customers and co-workers alike.

(Contrast this upbeat, infectiously cheerful Marge with the depressed, defeated woman she describes herself as being in the beginning of this chapter, after her husband's stroke!)

I heard folks in the booth next to ours reading aloud to each other the messages on the back of their checks: "There is joy and peace in knowing the Lord as your Savior," and, "You can share your burdens with the Lord."

Marge told us about two customers she had waited on earlier in the day. "I was beginning to get upset with them because they asked questions incessantly and made so many demands. Then I gave them their dinner checks with Scriptures on the back. When I returned to the table their attitudes had completely changed. It was remarkable how calm and courteous they had become. They told me they both had many problems and were very upset. When they read the Scriptures on their checks they felt comforted. I went in the back and wrote a short note to each of them. I told them, "God won't let you down."

At the end of our meal, my daughter and I looked at our checks and found, "Be quick to forgive others just as God has forgiven you," and "Blessed are the meek."

I asked Marge if I could share her story with other people. She hesitated at first. "I am totally unworthy to be held up as an example to other people," she said. "I make so many mistakes. I owe everything to my Lord and Savior, and He blesses me day by day. Since I accepted the Lord as my Savior, I'm not what I want to be, but praise God, I'm not what I used to be. I just pray every day that God will use me in my weakness, help me not to complain, and enable me to serve my customers as though I'm serving Him. The closer I get to Him the more I see how imperfect I am. I thank Him at least twice a day for my good health.

"I prayed that God would give me a ministry to other people, and He has. But He has also ministered to me in the process. I've become much closer to God as I've searched every day for Scriptures to give to others. God has been gradually building His Word into my heart every day."

I asked Marge for her favorite verse of Scripture.

"My favorite?" she said, smiling. "That's easy. Romans 8:28. 'All things work together for good to those who love God.' When life is hard and we are hurting we need to look back and remember what God has done. That gives us confidence for the future. I didn't doubt God when He was blessing me, why should I question Him when things don't go my way?"

....

THE FATHER'S HAND

While through this changing world below
I would not choose my path to go.
'Tis Father's hand that leadeth me,
Then O how safe His child must be.

Sometimes we walk in sunshine bright;
Sometimes in darkness of the night.
Sometimes the way I cannot see
But Father's hand still leadeth me.

Sometimes there seems no way to take,
But Father's hand a way doth make,
Sometimes I hear Him gently say,
"Come follow Me, this is the way."

Why should I mind the way I go?
His way is best for me, I know,
He is my strength, my truth, my way,
He is my comfort, rod and stay.

So on we travel hand in hand,
Bound for the heavenly promised land.
Always through all eternity,
I'll praise His name for leading me.

—Ida L. Cornett

How is the death of a father viewed through the eyes and emotions of children? Jim, who is now age 16, and his sister Stephanie, 19, recall the loss of their dad eight years ago.

The valuable lessons they learned and their keen insights will encourage children and teens adjusting to the loss of a parent. Parents, relatives, and friends will gain understanding of the child's perspective and be better equipped to help grieving children.

14

Jim and Stephanie's Story: LIFE WITHOUT DAD

For I am convinced that neither death nor life, neither angels nor demons, neither the present nor the future, nor any powers, neither height nor depth, nor anything else in all creation, will be able to separate us from the love of God that is in Christ Jesus our Lord.

Romans 8:38-39

MEMORIES OF LIFE WITH DAD

Stephanie:

Dad and I had a close relationship. We liked to play outside. We had devotions together in the evening that we called "talk and prayer time." He was a social worker and sometimes he took me with him to visit clients. I looked forward to going out for donuts every Saturday morning with him. We played a game of pretend call "Greg and Jan." We played together with my dolls and with little Fisher Price people. Because he died when I was eleven years of age I think I idealized much of what our relationship was. I think he died before I could see that he was a human being with faults.

Jim:

We had this great swing in our back yard. Daddy would push me very high until the ground seemed so far away that it was really scary, but he was always there to protect me from getting hurt. I enjoyed going out for donuts with him too. We talked to the guys at the donut shop and they always teased me about girl friends that I never had. One of my fond memories is of Daddy tying me on the back of his motorcycle so I would be safe and then taking me for a ride. What fun that was!

We spent time together playing sports in the back yard. We played a pretend game called "Pete and Joe." We would lie in bed on our sides facing each other. With match boxes we would make a little town between us and play together.

He was a caring father. When I looked back at Daddy after he died he was almost a God figure to me. I never saw his weaknesses. As a kid you think your dad is the greatest. And he was a great father. Oh, he would spank me occasionally, but I expected to be spanked when I disobeyed and that didn't lower my estimation of him.

Recollections of Dad's Illness

Jim:

One day Daddy walked out of the house and met Stephanie and me on the sidewalk. He didn't tell us he was going to die, but he told us he had cancer. Things began happening that made me realize Dad was very sick.

One evening my sister and Mom went to church. My mom said, "If there is any problem with Daddy, call 911."

Daddy woke up and asked, "Where is Grandpa?"

Grandpa had been there earlier and Daddy had been awake after he left, so that seemed like a strange question. Then he just kept rambling on about Grandpa. At times he would wake up and just start talking about things that didn't seem to make sense. I'd think, What is he talking about? I knew he was starting to get worse.

He told me to be the man of the family, take care of Mom, and be there for her. But I kept living in denial. I kept thinking, he'll come out of this. He'll be okay. Of course, the doctor gave us hope.

Earlier in his illness, Daddy's esophagus was surgically rebuilt. He seemed better and went back to work. He even went skiing, so I kept telling myself he would recover. Then he had a seizure and I became scared of him. It was weird. I was afraid to talk to my own father. Now I regret that I didn't lie by him, talk to him more, and spend more time with him while he was slowly dying.

Stephanie:

Dad took morphine for pain and that made him disoriented. I think that's why he said things that didn't make sense to Jimmy.

After he knew he had cancer, he said to me, "When a girl's father dies, she often looks for that fatherly love in the wrong places and can become 'boy crazy.' Don't become that way. Stay focused on school, good grades, and other good things."

Dad died within six months of telling us he had cancer. The deterioration was so fast. Mom had to help him take a shower and help with his other personal care. We saw a 200-pound man become a 90-pound person within six months. He was just a shell of himself when he died.

Responses of Others to Our Loss

Stephanie:

I remember a large crowd of people at the funeral and that made us feel good. Many people have difficulty knowing how to express their sympathy. They brought a casserole, or just said empty words. It seemed to meet their needs more than ours.

I remember standing in front of the casket and hearing people saying, "This is God's will." That didn't cut it for an eleven-year-old girl. People told me their stories of how their parents had died and then said, "Look at me. I made it and I turned out normal." We heard a lot of that kind of thing.We needed a comforting shoulder and someone saying, "I'm here for you if you need me." That would have been much better; but many people did not know what to say.

If you're going to say anything to someone who is grieving, think about what you are going to say before you say it. Be thoughtful, and consider what that person is feeling. Don't say the first thing that comes to mind. A lot of people said things to us, then realized that what they had said was foolish.

Jim:

I heard a man say to my cousin, "The first experience with a dead body is the worst!"

I felt like saying, "Why don't you just be quiet? That is not what we need to hear right now."

I needed friends to be with me, to put their arms around me and say, "I'm here for you if you want to talk."

I was really against crying. I guess it was my male ego. I didn't want Mom to cry at the funeral. I kept saying, "Don't cry!" I was very persistent with her about it. My friends didn't know how to handle my loss or what to say.

When I was eleven we moved to another city. My new friends did not know about my dad and I was glad because I despised pity. It made me feel weird to be with people who knew my dad had died and who thought they needed to be nice to us just because they felt sorry for us.

Stephanie:
There was a tremendous outpouring of love from our church. People invited us out to eat numerous times. Once we were invited out for breakfast, lunch, and dinner all in the same day and then someone invited us to go for ice cream that evening. Mom finally said, "This has to end. We are exhausted."

We were given an Amway get-away with exciting activities. Other families included us in their activities to keep us in a family structure. These were nice gestures and we appreciated them. Sometimes the things people did and the gifts they gave us seemed empty and non-caring. I think how you respond to another's loss should be based on the closeness of the relationship. It seems inappropriate for people who hardly know a child to expect him or her to share deep feelings with them. Perhaps they should bring the casseroles and stay a little more distant; but adults who are close to the child should make it known that they are willing to talk whenever the child feels the need.

Jim:
I remember sleeping in my mom's room during the summer. I woke up crying and she said, "We'll get through this." I remember lots and lots of food being brought to our house. The support we received from our friends was incredible.

Coping with Grief and Adjusting to Life Without Dad

Jim:
A father-son relationship is really special. Your dad is someone to hang out with, play catch with, and shoot baskets with. I never got to enjoy that luxury. I felt very angry at God, especially when I saw other boys playing with their dads. I felt jealous of my friend because he had a dad. That family included me in their activities and eventually I became good friends with the dad.

A friend of our family also did father-son kinds of activities with me, like golfing. I really appreciated him. He never did anything spectacular, but he spent time with me and I was grateful for his kindness.

I felt Stephanie was lucky compared with me. She still had that close relationship of daughter and Mom. I kept asking myself, What do I have? I didn't feel angry at her, but I did feel she had an advantage I didn't have.

I felt angry because God could have healed Dad, but He didn't. I never told anybody about it, but I had deep resentment toward the Lord for a long, long time. When my mom remarried, the anger became more intense. I thought, What is she trying to do, replace Daddy?

I'm not mad at God anymore. I spent a great deal of time thinking and trying to understand why God allowed Dad to die. I finally concluded that God had a bigger purpose and I just chilled out over time. I haven't figured out what that purpose is yet, but I'm learning to trust God's wisdom.

Stephanie:

Another family in our church seemed so perfect. I would see them on Sunday mornings with their dad. I thought, **Why do I have to go through this? Other girls my age don't have to.** I would see my friends at school who constantly fought with their fathers. I had a stepdad and I wondered why teenage girls and their fathers couldn't seem to get along. I would say to them, "Don't you understand how grateful you should be that you have your own father?"

Jim:

Anyone who says you can live a totally normal life after something like this is entirely wrong. My life is never going to be the same. I have this feeling that if I could live through Dad's illness again, I would do things differently. I wish I had spent more time with him. At other times when I reflect on it, I realize that I didn't know anything like this was going to happen. Why should I have spent more time with my dad than any other kid?

Stephanie:

I felt overwhelmed that Jim didn't have a father anymore. I felt responsible to do something about it because I was convinced that it was not good for a boy to grow up with two women and no man in the house. Boys need a strong male influence in their lives.

Jim:

I suggest prayer for other children going through the loss of a parent because prayer helped me through it. It sounds simple. Just talking to God about my feelings and the things I didn't understand. Talk about it with other people. Talk about the good times and even the bad times. Get that out of your system. Because if you keep that bottled up you are going to be very sorry when you grow older.

Another thing: Be sure to let yourself cry about it. Don't keep it inside. For a long time I didn't feel there was anyone I could just talk to and get the emotion out.

Stephanie:
There were times I wanted to talk about it, but I didn't have anyone I felt would listen. There were other times I didn't want to talk but others wanted me to share my feelings.

In my family, we romanticize my father. He was a great man, I won't deny that, but every time we talk about him it's only good things. We never mention the times he yelled at us. I think we need to realize more of his humanness. I spent the first few years just not coping with it. I kept it bottled up because I didn't want to share it, and I didn't think I could really find anyone who could relate to my situation.

When I was in high school and my mom remarried, there was so much to cope with that I didn't care whether they related or not. I had to talk to someone. I spoke with my high school counselors many times and some religion teachers. They were willing to listen. "Just talk," they said, "and we won't judge you for what you say."

There were also times I became very tired of rehashing everything about my father. I wanted to put him to rest and get on with my life. But later I realized it was good that we talked incessantly about him and didn't cover up the fact that he was dead.

Jim:
I used to talk to friends and they would be unresponsive. But I felt it was better than talking to a brick wall about it. I even talked to my dog. He was a big help! That sounds really strange, but that dog was a great counselor. He'd listen to everything I had to say, and he'd never interrupt.

My dog died not too long ago. I knew him longer than I knew my Dad because we had him twelve years. He was part of the family and he was my friend.

I kept my feelings bottled up for a long time. The only person I was close enough to share my feelings with was my mom and she was going through the same thing I was. I didn't think it would help to talk with her because she was probably feeling the very same things we were.

My grandpa died not long ago at the age of 91. At his funeral I thought, I'm old enough to cry. I'm with people who love me. I'm going to cry, and I don't care what anybody thinks. I wasn't wise enough to realize it was okay to cry at my dad's funeral, when I was eight years old.

It seems like an oxymoron that God helped me the most even though I hated Him the most. He used other people to help me get through the grief, and to realize that life goes on.

Our uncle was a big help also. He had lost his mother when he was young. He was like a big sponge. He was there to absorb all the tears and soak up all my problems. Our relatives were very supportive.

Stephanie:
What helped me was becoming aware that many people were suffering a lot worse than I was and if they could survive then I surely could too. I love to read, and I always try to find a character in each book that shares a situation similar to mine. It comforted me after Dad died to relate to characters in books who could share the pain I was feeling.

The Impact of This Loss on our Faith

Stephanie:
I attribute the strengthening of my faith to my father's death. Romans 8:38-39 was my dad's favorite verse. It comforted me to know that nothing could separate me from God's love.

I now realize that we are completely at God's mercy, and whatever happens to us in our lives can bring us closer to God if we have the right attitude. You have to have faith in Him. If you don't, what do you have?

We are too earthbound. We are all too geared into this world. Instead, we should be more focused on eternity, because this earthly life just doesn't last.

Jim:
A lot of kids get closer to God as they grow up, but not many of them have a dramatic experience as we did that challenged our faith. I grew closer to God through this loss. My friend's dad died a year ago. He doesn't like God, Christianity, or anything related to it. Some kids don't know about God and don't have the Christian influence we had that helped us grow closer to Him.

Mom's Remarriage

Jim:
Mom remarried three and a half years after Dad died. I was eleven and in the sixth grade. Stephanie was fourteen and in the ninth grade. Before she got married, Mom said something important to me. "I will always love Daddy, even if I remarry," she said. "I will not remarry unless you say it is all right."

Bill, the man she wanted to marry, asked permission also. I gave them my permission to get married. I said it was okay. One thing I thought about was that we couldn't keep living on coupons and social security the rest of our lives. And my mom needed a husband; she was lonely. I was trying to consider what my mom needed.

Stephanie:

I wasn't excited about it at all. My dad had only been dead three years and I thought, This is happening so quickly. Can't Mom wait until I am older? I didn't like the idea, because I knew I would have to move.

Once I told my friends I was moving, I felt shunned and mistreated by them. They said, "We won't see her in high school anyway, so what's the point of spending a lot of time with her now?" Junior highers can be mean.

Now that I look back on it I am glad that we did move. I enjoy our new location.

Adjusting to a Stepparent

Jim:

If your parent asks permission to remarry, do what you think in your heart is right. Think beyond the present situation to what is best for the future. Think about other people. Life isn't just about pleasing yourself. It's about pleasing your parents and pleasing God. You can't just do everything for yourself.

When I agreed to Mom's remarriage I didn't do it for myself. I did it for my mom. I'm glad I did it now.

Stephanie:

I think it's always hard not to compare our stepfather with our father. We were really young when we knew our dad. We saw him as perfect. When Mom remarried, Jimmy and I were mature enough to see that this new man was a human being with faults. He wasn't anything like we remembered our biological father. It's hard not to compare them.

Jim:

I've never thought of Bill as a father. I've thought of him as a real close friend. He's a pal. He's not a father figure to me. We do not call him "Dad." Instead, we call him, "Bill."

Stephanie:

I know a girl whose father died when she was in eighth grade. She is a college freshman now and her mother has not remarried for those five years. She and her mother had grown very close. It was hard for the mom to be left alone when her daughter moved away to attend college in another state. I am glad to know that my mom has someone with her and I am not responsible for her and her happiness. She has another friend now.

Remarriage does not solve all problems. It hasn't for any of us. Some people paint a rosy picture that is just not true. Don't expect things to be as they were in your initial family. Try not to compare. Accept the fact that it will be different. Because we were older when Bill married Mom, I think of his relationship to me as a friend. We don't pretend that it is a dad-to-daughter relationship, which it isn't.

Jim:

This was a package deal. When Bill married Mom he married us too. He has coped with it well. If you compare your present family with your previous one, you will never be happy. Other kids should not think this new man is going to replace their dad. No one is ever going to replace him. Just be happy that God sent someone else into your life to help ease the pain a little.

Bill has helped ease the pain. He's real supportive.

Don't have unrealistic expectations. In fact, don't expect anything. Be happy with what you get. Make the most of the present.

....

GOD EVER CARES

GOD EVER CARES! Not only in life's summer
When skies are bright and days are long and glad,
He cares as much when life is draped in winter,
And heart doth feel bereft, and lone, and sad.

GOD EVER CARES! His heart is ever tender.
His love doth never fail nor show decay.
The loves of earth, though strong and deep, may perish,
But His shall never, never pass away.

GOD EVER CARES! And thus when life is lonely,
When blessings one time prized are growing dim,
The heart may find a sweet and sunny shelter—
A refuge and a resting place in Him.

GOD EVER CARES! And time can never change Him.
His nature is to care, and love, and bless.
And drearest, darkest, emptiest days afford Him
But means to make more sweet His own caress.

—J. Danson Smith

Holly became a widow at age 30, and was left with a nine-year-old daughter to raise. Her husband died at age 39 from a massive heart attack.

God was Holly's faithful Refuge as she picked up the fragments of her once-happy life and trudged forward in faith, learning to trust God in ever deeper ways.

15

Holly's Story:
HOPE FOR A YOUNG WIDOW

Because of the Lord's great love we are not consumed,
for his compassions never fail.
They are new every morning;
great is your faithfulness.

Lamentations 3:22-23

I walked into the hospital to visit my husband, David, who had been admitted the day before. He was not in his room. "Where is he?" I asked a nurse in the hallway.

She didn't answer.

"Where is he?" I half-demanded, half-pleaded. "Tell me now! Has he had a heart attack?"

"Yes," she said, "he had a heart attack. He's in the Intensive Care Unit."

I rushed to the ICU, and the instant I walked through the door, a nurse put her arms around me and asked, "Is there anyone I can call for you? Your husband's condition is very grave. We are making arrangements to transfer him by helicopter to another hospital."

I had no warning; no indication how serious David's condition was prior to this. He had been treated for bronchitis and ulcers; but he was an unusually strong man, appeared healthy, and always worked hard. Because of economic conditions, David had been laid off from his job several times. The last unemployment lasted two years so he decided to start a business of his own. Being the boss was not easy for him, and he often became frustrated and angry from the pressure of employee problems. Perhaps the stress affected his heart.

One week before this sudden turn for the worse, he had been admitted to the hospital for nothing more serious than to determine the cause of poor circulation in his foot. He had injured that foot during military duty in Viet Nam. But during the examination, some unusual heart symptoms showed up. Two doctors argued right in front of David as to whether or not he had suffered a heart attack. They wanted to transfer him to another hospital for additional testing. David became angry at what he perceived was a lack of competence by the doctors and he refused to stay in the hospital.

Yesterday, one week after that incident, I persuaded him to return to the hospital to find out if he had heart problems that needed treatment. While there, he had experienced a heart attack.

I was stunned by the news. How could my big, strong, healthy husband have had a life-threatening heart attack with no warning symptoms? It seemed impossible.

"TILL DEATH DO US PART . . . "

David was transferred by helicopter and my sister-in-law and I traveled two and a half hours by car. As we drove, I kept thinking, Why are we driving fast? He isn't going to live through this. Then I began arguing with myself, Don't even think that way! Think positively!

When we arrived at the hospital, the doctor came out to explain David's treatment and condition.

"May I go in with him," I asked?

"No, I can't allow you in the emergency room right now," he replied.

I felt so guilty. I kept thinking, **I'm not where I need to be. During our ten years of marriage we have gone through everything together and now, when it comes to the most important crisis we have ever faced, I am letting David down.**

Less than two hours after we arrived at the hospital the doctor appeared again. I knew from the expression on his face that the news was not good. He pulled a chair right up in front of me and sat down. Then, taking both my hands in his, he looked right into my eyes and said, "David didn't make it."

I felt totally numb. I couldn't even cry. I sat staring at the wall. He squeezed my hands and I focused my eyes on him again.

"May I see him?" I asked.

"In a few minutes," he replied.

What happened next made an indelible imprint on my memory. The doctor and nurse went with me into the room. The doctor put his arms around me and stood there holding me and crying with me. I couldn't get over it. Here was this doctor who never saw David or me before and he cared enough to cry with me. I will never forget it.

On the way home I tried to think, in the midst of my shock, pain, and confusion, what I must do next. I began to select pall bearers. When I arrived home I learned that the funeral details had already been taken care of by our family. I did select the cemetery plot, but even in the midst of my grief, I wanted to be a part of all the decisions that involved my husband. I felt hurt, although I realized our family was trying their best to help me. They did an excellent job with all of it. I couldn't have asked for more compassion and help than our family gave me.

The minister who had married us conducted David's funeral service. Years earlier, we had promised before God that we would love each other "till death do us part," and we had kept that promise.

DEALING WITH ANGER AND OTHER EMOTIONS

The autopsy showed multiple heart damage from previous silent heart attacks. I felt very angry at the doctors who missed the diagnosis completely. I kept asking "What if—?" And I kept thinking, If only—

I became extremely angry at David for refusing to stay in the hospital the week before he died, and for not submitting to the tests. I went to the cemetery and talked to him as if he could hear me. "I'm so angry at you, David," I said. "Why did you leave me? Why didn't you take care of yourself? Why didn't you do what the doctors wanted you to? How could you do this to me? How could you leave me to raise our daughter alone?"

I never had the chance to tell David good-bye, and I told him the things I wanted to tell him there at the cemetery. Gradually the anger subsided as I realized that God was in control and I couldn't change what had already happened. Even though I didn't understand, maybe it was all God's plan and I had to trust Him.

I was comforted by the Serenity Prayer:

> God grant me the serenity
> To accept the things I cannot change,
> The courage to change the things I can,
> And the wisdom to know the difference.
> Amen.

My loneliness was intense. After my daughter, Melissa, went to school each day I would leave the house. I could not make myself stay there alone, so for the first three or four months I thought of every excuse I could to go away. I did a lot of window shopping, driving around, and visiting my mom and dad. Nights were especially difficult. I could count on one hand the number of nights David and I had been apart in our ten years of marriage, and the emptiness I felt was nearly unbearable. I would watch television and read until three or four in the morning. Then when it was time to start the day I wouldn't want to get out of bed. I kept asking, "What is there to get up for?" I would see Melissa off to school and go back to bed, sometimes until noon.

I read many books on grief and about heart attacks. I needed to understand what had happened to David. **Instantly A Widow** touched me as no other book. I felt as if I was reading my story in print. The feelings and struggles so closely echoed my own.

My church family helped me in many ways, but I had a need they didn't really know how to deal with. Because I was a widow at age thirty, I didn't fit in anywhere. All the other adults were either older widows or married couples. Eventually I became involved in a church Bible study and worked with the children of the Bible study participants. This gave me contact with others and a sense of being needed.

One day I saw a bookmark with the poem, "Don't Quit" on it. I felt inspired to keep going on by the words. I bought the bookmark and read the poem over and over.

DON'T QUIT

> When things go wrong, as they sometimes will,
> And the road you're trudging seems all uphill,
> When the funds are low, and the debts are high,
> And you want to smile, but you have to sigh,
> When care is pressing you down a bit,
> Rest if you must, but don't you quit.
>
> Life is queer with its twists and turns,
> As every one of us sometimes learns.

And many a failure turns about,
When he might have won had he stuck it out.
Don't give up though the pace seems slow,
You may succeed with another blow.

Success is failure turned inside out,
The silver tint of the clouds of doubt,
And you never can tell how close you are,
It may be near when it seems so far,
So stick in the fight when you're hardest hit,
Its when things seem worst,
That you must not quit.

—Author unknown

Life and death often involve some very strange coincidences.

I often turned to my brother-in-law for help with financial and legal issues. Then he died—twenty-three months to the day after David died, and in the very same hospital room where David died. David's mother had also been a patient in that room, just a few months after David's death. On the occasions when my mother-in-law and my brother-in-law were hospitalized there, I found it very hard to enter that room again. I couldn't have stood it without God's help.

THE FAITHFULNESS OF GOD

As I reflect on my three years as a widow I realize how faithful God was to me. Melissa and I never went hungry; we always had clothes to wear and gas for the car. We had to decide many times what we would use the gas for: Should we go grocery shopping or save the gas to drive to church?

David had not paid any income tax for the year he died and I received two huge bills for federal and state tax. Again God provided through Social Security, and I was able to pay the tax bills in monthly payments.

Melissa had been very close to her father and she was having a difficult time coping with his death. I felt she needed me at home to provide security and love, so I did not work outside our home. God made it possible for me to stay home with her.

I will never forget that first Christmas without David. There was a small church two miles from us; they adopted us and brought delicious food and lovely gifts. In addition, someone from our own church adopted us and showered us with presents. It was a wonderful outpouring of God's love to us through these kind people.

God met our spiritual needs through His Word and prayer. One of the Scriptures God used to comfort me was 2 Corinthians 4:8-9—"We are hard pressed on every side, but not crushed; perplexed, but not in despair; persecuted, but not abandoned; struck down, but not destroyed."

My relationship with God has grown closer and deeper through this time of grief and recovery. It has become a daily walk with Him, a daily dependence upon Him for all our needs, rather than only in times of crisis. The devotional booklet, **Our Daily Bread,** has been an important resource for me, and it often seemed that many of the readings in that devotional were prepared just for me. I began to read the Bible regularly and was comforted by constantly listening to the music and messages on Family Life radio. So I'm grateful to God for the way He has drawn me closer to Himself after my loss, but I'm even more grateful for what God has done in my daughter's life.

Six months after her Dad's death, Melissa accepted the Lord Jesus as her Savior.

A BIG STEP

Exactly seventeen months after David's death, I took a big step in moving on with my life. I took my wedding rings off and put them away.

For months, friends had been saying to me, "Holly, you must take your wedding rings off! How do you expect to find someone else if you are wearing wedding rings? No one will know you're available!" On this one particular day, I thought about that advice a lot. All day long, Ecclesiastes 3:1-4 kept going through my mind. I opened my Bible several times during the day and read it:

> There is a time for everything,
>   and a season for every activity under heaven:
> a time to be born and a time to die,
>   a time to plant and a time to uproot,
> a time to kill and a time to heal,
>   a time to tear down and a time to build,
> a time to weep and a time to laugh,
>   a time to mourn and a time to dance,

I felt God was saying, "It is time to laugh again. Your hard grief is over and it is time to go on. It's time to open a new chapter in your life and start rebuilding." I was sobbing and tears were flowing down my cheeks, but I took my rings off, placed them tenderly in a box and put them away. It was time for me to do this, but nobody can tell another grieving person when it is time for them to make decisions. Every person has to grieve in his or her own way, and must recover in his or her own time.

God reinforced that message through Isaiah 43:18, "Forget the former things; do not dwell on the past." He was reminding me not to get stuck in the past, but to move forward, trusting Him.

This was a turning point in my grief. From that day I began to rebuild my life. I realized that the beautiful memories of my happy life with David could never be erased, and he would want me to be happy now.

WHAT I LEARNED

Perhaps one good thing that will come of this painful experience in my life is that I will be able to share with others some of what I learned during the shock and grieving process of my loss. Here are a few suggestions I have for other young widows:

Stay involved in your local church.

Find some good listeners who will allow you to talk through your feelings and not judge you. Don't keep emotions bottled up!

Read the Bible and pray regularly.

Write down your feelings. It really helped me to keep a diary. I filled two huge journals with conversations I had with God. I continue to write in a notebook, and my journaling has been a great source of comfort to me. In it I write Bible verses that have special meaning, quotes from my devotional readings, verses from songs, and poems that inspire me.

If you want to help someone who is grieving, my counsel to you would be to help that person to feel included and wanted. David and I had good friends that we were with nearly every weekend. The men fished together, and we all played games and shared pizza together. There were children Melissa's age and they were close friends. After David died they assured me, "We won't let our relationship change." But I never heard from them. I would hear that they were planning a party, but I was never invited. They rejected me because I wasn't a couple any more. Melissa and I felt labeled as "different." We didn't fit in anymore, even with the friends who had been so close. And that hurt.

The church tried to be supportive, but there wasn't any program to really meet my needs as a very young widow with a child. People made promises to Melissa to take her bowling, out to eat, and to the museum. Most of those promises were not kept. Melissa felt hurt and rejected. So I would caution not to make promises you don't intend to keep, especially to children.

A NEW LIFE

My father was in poor health for many years. We had a close relationship. As he grew older, I thought about the uncertainty of life without him, and I would be comforted by the song, "I Know Who Holds Tomorrow." After David's death that song became even more significant. It reminded me that God is in control, and no matter what happens, He will always be with me.

Dad was especially supportive after David's death. He worried about the many needs I had as a single parent. He was in his seventies and thought about the future when he would not be here to help me. I know now that Dad didn't need to worry, because God had a plan. Of course, at that time, I was worried about the future myself. In fact, after David died, I thought my world had ended. I had my mind made up never to marry again.

God changed my thinking when He brought a wonderful man into my life, and we were married just four months before my dad died. God brought him to me at just the right time to give me support and encouragement after the loss of my loving father. Our marriage has been good for Melissa also. She is developing a close relationship with her stepdad.

Church friends have told me, "I admire the strength you've shown, Holly. I have watched you mature through this experience, and I just don't know how I could handle a tragedy like yours." I remind them that my strength comes from God. I can't even imagine making it through the grief without Him.

My mother suggested several times that I write my story to encourage others. It seemed impossible for me to write a book. When I was asked to be interviewed for this book, I wished I could tell my mother about it. She's in heaven now, and I think she would be very pleased.

....

NOT NOW, BUT IN THE COMING YEARS

Not now, but in the coming years,
    It may be in the better land,
We'll read the meaning of our tears,
    And then, some time, we'll understand.

Then trust in God through all thy days,
    Fear not, for He doth hold thy hand.
Though dark the way, still sing and praise,
    Some time, up there, we'll understand.

—M.N. Cornelius

Walk alongside Beverly and feel her pain as she shares the rejection she experienced in response to her brother's gay lifestyle and AIDS diagnosis. Then rejoice with her as she relates her life-changing encounter with unconditional love demonstrated to her dying brother.

16

Beverly's Story:
LONGING FOR LOVE

For God so loved the world that he gave his one and only Son,
that whoever believes in him shall not perish but have eternal life.

John 3:16

An atmosphere of unconditional love was lacking in the family where I grew up. In our family, we did not discuss real feelings and issues with each other very much. Our mother was absent from home a lot of the time, sometimes because she was in school, and often because of illness. Our father spent as much time with us as he could. I was eleven years older than my brother, Jon. Because Mom was absent much of the time I became Jon's "second mom."

I remember Jon as a happy, active child even though Dad was never involved in sports or other typical father-son activities with him. I married when Jon was seven years old. He told me in later years that he knew something was wrong with him when he was nine years of age, but he never told anyone. He was afraid to tell anyone because he was sure he would be rejected by family and friends if they knew he had homosexual feelings.

Jon had been brought up in the church, was a Christian, and loved the Lord. Even though his relationship with me had been a close one, he didn't share his concern with me because I was married and busy with my own family. During his teenage years he was very active in the church, serving as youth leader, singing in the choir, and playing piano. After graduating from high school he traveled with a Christian musical group for two years. He tried dating girls but was never able to enter into a meaningful love relationship with any of them. At times he felt a desire to have children and he thought of trying to hide his homosexuality within a heterosexual marriage.

After two years with the musical group he moved to another state. The move was a bad decision because he became influenced by the wrong kind of friends and his Christian walk deteriorated. He was friendly, he was a great cook who enjoyed entertaining, and he loved playing the piano, planting flowers, and going camping. He found a job as waiter in a restaurant, and worked his way up to the head waiter position, which included being in charge of banquets and conferences.

When Jon told me he was gay, I responded with a letter urging him to go to counseling and to leave the homosexual lifestyle. I quoted lots of Scripture references that I thought were words of encouragement, and added, "I am here for you. You can get out of this." Jon did not see this as encouragement at all. Instead, he interpreted my response as preaching to him. He became very angry and withdrew from our family for an entire year.

"You loved me."

Eventually Jon made contact by phone and visited us several times. Then he suffered a devastating loss: During one three-month period, seven of his friends died of AIDS. Jon was shattered, and he cried with me about them. "I'll always be here for you, Jon," I told him. "Whenever you need me, I'll always love you and be here to help you any way I can."

He started to clean up his life and began going from church to church looking for one that would accept him. The result was total rejection and condemnation. He felt completely forsaken and abandoned by God's people.

I regret that I never went to visit him. I didn't realize how great his needs were and what kind of conditions he was living in. When he became ill with AIDS and I did go to see him, I was shocked by his unkempt living conditions. As the disease took its toll, he had very little energy to keep his house clean. He conserved every ounce of energy in order to work and support himself. My heart ached as I realized how much he needed the love and support that had been lacking in our family.

I wanted to do all I could during his remaining days, and I spent most of the last four months of his life with him, trying to be an encourager and to look after his needs. At the same time, I had a husband and three children, so there were numerous six hundred-mile trips back and forth, during which I felt completely stressed out trying to balance my brother's desperate needs and my home responsibilities. As I approached the point of exhaustion, both physically and emotionally, Jon became increasingly weak.

By this time, he was receiving hospice care. His digestion began failing and he was kept alive with intravenous feedings. Eventually his weight dropped to eighty pounds and he was wearing diapers. I held him and cried, thinking of all the times I had held him when I was eleven or twelve and he was a baby in diapers. Jon's short life had come full-circle, and here I was, holding him again, trying to comfort him as his life slipped away before my eyes. There was nothing I could do to keep him from dying.

I felt terrible guilt because it seemed our family had failed Jon. I kept thinking that his life could have been saved from this tragedy if we had adequately met his need for love, communication, and support. Three weeks before he died I shared the guilt I was feeling. Tentatively, I asked, "Do you know why you have this sexual orientation? I mean . . . do you think I might have been responsible? Was it something about the way I raised you when Mother wasn't available?"

"No," he said. "I'm sure you had nothing to do with it. You loved me. You held me, rocked me, took care of me, and baked my birthday cakes. You were the person who made me feel loved when we were growing up together."

ACCEPTED AT LAST

Those last few weeks with Jon changed my life. I observed unconditional love in action, love as I had never known it before. I saw loving, supportive people from the hospice who modeled unconditional love to Jon.

A Christian lady presented him with a beautiful silk robe she had made and a song she had written especially for him. That song was used at Jon's funeral. She presented me with a corsage and I felt accepted and loved by her.

I will never forget Stan, Jon's Jewish friend, who came at 3:00 a.m., as soon as he knew Jon was so ill. He sat beside Jon on the bed, holding his hands and offering comfort and kindness. I was greatly impressed as I watched this compassionate man offering encouragement by his presence and touch to Jon's thin, disease-ridden body.

My saddest moment came about a week before his death when Jon asked me to help him with the weights on his legs so he could walk. It was a crushing disappointment to realize that he could not walk. It was then that the horrible reality began to sink in that the disease had taken over and the end was in sight. The grief washed over me.

Here was my brother, a person created in God's image and yet shunned for much of his adult life by those who called themselves Christians. I wondered, How would Christ have responded to Jon? Would He have turned away from him like so many Christians have? Or would He have treated Jon just as He treated lepers, adulterers, tax collectors, and thieves? With love and acceptance, confronting their sin yet loving their souls and healing their hearts?

I ached for the years of pain Jon had endured as he longed for love and acceptance. Having been a "mother" as well as a sister to Jon in his early years, I felt I was losing my child as well as my brother.

Jon's last wish was that he not be alone for Easter, so I stayed with him, living and sleeping in his hospital room. The sadness and helplessness overwhelmed me at times as I realized how close I was to losing him forever. Jon wanted to go Easter shopping, so I took him to the mall in the wheelchair.

Just eight days before Jon's death, his friend Stan, and I took him to his last Easter service. After the service we wheeled Jon to the front of the church to visit with the pastor. Jon told me he had made his peace with God and longed to be accepted into the fellowship of a church. He had been allowed to speak regarding AIDS in this church. Earlier in the spring I participated in a panel discussion in that church along with two doctors. I spoke about my personal experience with my brother's disease and the doctors addressed the medical aspect. The pastor had visited Jon in the hospital and modeled Christ's unconditional love. I will never forget the beautiful smile that illuminated Jon's entire face when the pastor shook his hand after the Easter service and told him how glad he was to have him there.

Just one week before Jon died I was able to tell him that he had been accepted by that church as a member. This was the only church out of the many he visited that accepted him, and not until he was on his death bed. I will always treasure the memory of the radiant smile that broke over his face when I gave him the news. That smile reflected his joy at finally feeling love and acceptance from the church.

The Monday after Easter, before going back home, I told Jon he didn't have to hold on any longer. The only things keeping him alive were his mind and intravenous feedings. The following Sunday Jon talked to me by phone and told me he was having the intravenous tubes taken out Monday.

My last conversation with Jon was three hours before he died on Tuesday. I talked with him, told him I loved him, and that I was on my way to be with him.

He was gone before I arrived.

ISOLATION, REJECTION, SILENCE

The funeral was a tremendous outpouring of comfort, love, and caring from the people at hospice and that one church. It lasted one and a half hours. I played one of the songs, "I've Been With Jesus," Jon had played so skillfully on the piano and I tried to do the song in Jon's style. I played "Amazing Grace," as we all sang together. I related Jon's story and thanked the people for their outpouring of love. God gave me special strength to participate in the funeral. I felt no rejection whatsoever that day because of my brother's past lifestyle and disease.

When I returned home, however, I was shocked by the attitudes which confronted me. A number of people told me, "You should have disowned your brother. He chose his lifestyle, he knew the consequences, and he deserved what he got. You should not have neglected your own family to care for your wayward brother. AIDS was God's punishment for his sin."

Many Christian people kept their distance from me after that. They seemed to avoid contact with me because I had touched someone with AIDS. I felt humiliated and isolated. My friends—including my Christian friends—turned their backs on me. The phone was silent. Even my husband didn't want to hear my feelings. I had no support during my grief, no one to talk to about my feelings.

I began to wonder if I could have been infected by the HIV virus, even though I knew that infection by casual contact is virtually impossible. The fact that other people treated me as a contaminated person probably contributed to my own fears. I finally convinced myself to be tested for the HIV virus. I walked into the lab and immediately felt the icy attitude there. I felt I was being treated as something less than a human, more like a lump of dirt. I started to cry.

It was hard to speak, but I finally said to the lab technician with trembling lips, "My brother died of AIDS and I want to be tested just to be sure I didn't contract it." Her attitude toward me—which had been clearly judgmental—immediately changed when she learned I wasn't there because of some behavioral connection with AIDS, such as intravenous drug use. I thought, Is this how it feels to be a drug addict or a homosexual? Is this what it's like to be judged and condemned by people you come in contact with? If I were an addict or a homosexual, would that make me less than human? I'm still a creature of God created by Him in His image.

Two months to the day after Jon's death, my mother died. We didn't always have a close relationship and she seemed to feel jealous at times because I had a better relationship with Jon than she did. She loved Jon and had an extremely difficult time dealing with his homosexuality. I think it would be accurate to say that she died of a broken heart. Her health was poor and the grief over Jon's death surpassed her ability to cope.

UP FROM DEPRESSION

I was at the bottom of a deep well of depression, struggling to come to terms with two major losses in my life. I knew I couldn't handle the emotional pain alone, especially in view of how isolated my life had become, so I decided to seek outside help. My first step was to make an appointment with my doctor for a medical examination. Next I joined a support group. Then I started exercising and found that feeling well physically helped me deal more effectively with the emotional upheaval.

In spite of my intense grief, I sensed an inner peace that surprised me. My spiritual strength was renewed through my Bible reading. Some of my favorite passages during that time were:

> But those who hope in the LORD
> will renew their strength.
> They will soar on wings like eagles;
> they will run and not grow weary,
> they will walk and not be faint.
> Isaiah 40:31

> . . . Because God has said,
> "Never will I leave you;
> never will I forsake you."
> Hebrews 13:5

> The LORD is my Shepherd . . .
> Psalm 23:1

I kept telling myself, I will trust God! I felt comforted through prayer and by the music as I played the piano in church and sang in the choir. I phoned the friends I had made while staying with Jon. They were far away, but they were the only people I could find who would supportively allow me to share my feelings.

Finally, about three and a half months after Jon's death, my friends and family realized I needed to talk. The emotions bottled up inside me had nearly reached the bursting point. I found a couple of friends to share fun times with. They would also listen patiently and let me drift into and out of my pain over Mother's and Jon's death, and they didn't judge me for my feelings.

God used the circumstances surrounding Jon's death to teach me that He loves me unconditionally. As I saw Him reaching out to Jon through the nonjudgmental love of others, I began to realize how great His love is for me. He helped me realize that I don't have to perform perfectly in order to gain His favor, that His love is constant, and He doesn't cast me off when I sin. He accepts my confession, and He forgives and continues to love me. I feel such a peace, acceptance, and freedom from guilt in my relationship with God.

My friends tell me they also see a change in my attitude toward others. I am learning to love others unconditionally as a result of my experience. For the first time in my life I am able to thank God for my emotionally handicapped, hearing-impaired, seventeen-year-old child.

LOVE IN ACTION

My advice to others who are dealing with AIDS victims is not to let them see the fear you may have of contracting their disease. Love them, hug and touch them. Don't make them feel like outcasts or lepers. Try to give as much of yourself to them as you can. Sometimes just sitting with them is what they need most. Bring their favorite foods even if they can only eat a few bites. And eat with them. Do everything you can to make them feel special. Rent their favorite videos. Bring a cool drink to quench their thirst in a fancy crystal stem glass—even ice water seems special served in that fashion! Ask if a back rub would be soothing to them. Above all, don't let them see your fear.

To those who wish to help the family members of the AIDS victims, I suggest that you ask, "Would you like to talk about it? How are you feeling?" Assure them you want to help and be a friend who doesn't judge. Show God's unconditional love.

This experience has made me a stronger Christian with increased confidence in God. He is sustaining me with His peace, which is promised in Isaiah 26:3, "You will keep in perfect peace him whose mind is steadfast, because he trusts in you."

....

HE IS ABLE

He is able—more than able
    to accomplish what concerns me today.
He is able—more than able
    to handle anything that comes my way.
He is able—more than able
    to do much more than I could ever dream.
He is able—more than able
    to make me what He wants me to be.

—Gary Ferguson and Rory Noland

It has been exciting to watch God draw these special people into my life, and bring their stories together for this book.

Now, some concluding reflections to weave the strands of their stories into a larger tapestry of healing and recovery ...

17

Concluding Thoughts:
OUR BEST COMFORTER

As I approached the writing of this book, I prayed that God would direct me to the people whose stories He wanted included. It has been exciting to watch Him work in answer to my prayer. He has directed me to a number of wonderful people, some I probably would not have otherwise met. I shed many tears as I listened to recollections of broken hearts that have been healed by the God of all comfort. Then I attempted to distill each of their stories from their own words and present them in a way that would offer hope and help to you, the reader.

Each person's experience is unique and complements the others, while offering a glimpse into the strength and consolation that only comes from God. What can we learn from these experiences? What common threads of truth are woven through each one? There are many insights collected in these pages, but let's focus on just five:

1. Life is fragile.

We have read this truth lettered on plaques, worked in cross stitch, and repeated in sermons and everyday conversations again and again. We all know it is true, but nothing can teach us that truth more clearly than to lose someone we love. It helps us recognize that our focus in life should be on eternal things: on living out the truth of God's Word, and on loving and building relationships with people.

On the bedroom wall on the farm where we grew up, my sister and I had a plaque which read,

Only one life, 'twill soon be past,
Only what's done for Christ will last.

Facing the death of a loved one forces us to ask, "Why am I here and what should I accomplish with the remainder of my life?" Coming face to face with death forces us—as it did Sharon (Chapter 11: Father to the Fatherless)—to put our lives in proper perspective and establish appropriate priorities.

Marge, John, and Holly gained comfort from the precious memories stored in their memory banks. They encourage us to build happy memories with our remaining loved ones. We need to slow down, smell the flowers, go on a picnic, sit in the porch swing, enjoy a sunset together, and share all the memorable experiences we can with those we love. This very day could be our last together. James 4:14 tell us "you do not even know what will happen tomorrow. What is your life? You are a mist that appears for a little while and then vanishes." When we have a clearer sense of the fragility and brevity of life, we can live it with greater intensity—and deeper joy.

2. Each person's grief experience is unique.

The way we respond to the loss of a loved one depends on several factors:

First, **temperament.** Some of us are easy-going; others are more serious and things hurt us more deeply.

Second, the **length and closeness of the relationship** with the loved one. Loving calls for great courage, for in loving we always risk getting hurt. The tears we shed and the pain we feel after a loss testify to the depth of our love.

Third, the **circumstances of the death.** In the case of a prolonged terminal illness, the grieving process often begins long before the loved one dies, as we saw in June's experience. When death finally comes, relief often accompanies the shock. The grieving period in such cases is often a time of slow, gradual recovery.

But when a loved one dies from unexpected, violent causes, such as murder, suicide, or accident, the shock, denial, and panic may last for many months, as illustrated by Sharon's experience following the plane crash. The grieving period is often a time of tumultuous emotions and upheaval.

Each person needs to grieve in his or her own way, and find recovery in his or her own time.

3. Having loving, caring people in your life is essential to recovery from grief.

Each of these stories points out the value of supportive, nonjudgmental, willing listeners. Friends who give us the gift of their time and attention can speed the emotional healing process, and can even help us avoid the physical illness that often come from keeping toxic emotions stuffed down inside us. In a time of loss, we need patient, available people who will say, "I'm here for you, at any time, for any reason." We need to be reminded when the grief is fresh, "Let the tears flow and give yourself time."

Tears and time are two essentials for the healing of our pain. Equally essential are good friends who will encourage us to maintain our health through adequate rest, regular exercise, nourishing food, and necessary medical attention. The path to grief recovery is smoother when we are physically strong.

Galatians 6:2 bids us, "Carry each other's burdens, and in this way you will fulfill the law of Christ." The stories in this book point to the many ways we can carry one another's burdens and ease the pain of loss by giving emotional support and practical encouragement.

The pain of loss is always traumatic. But as our emotional trauma begins to subside, we can help to heal our own grief by reaching out with compassion and kindness to others who are hurting. Several stories point out the therapeutic value of helping others as we journey through grief.

4. Trials can bring us closer to God.

Faith is the stabilizing factor that helped each of these people grieve more effectively. They were helped by the conviction that God was with them and would bring them through. Our faith can be greatly strengthened by adversity as these stories demonstrate. That is why the psalmist could say, "It was good for me to be afflicted so that I might learn your decrees" (Psalm 119:71).

Sorrow and loss are painful, and our natural tendency is to shrink from that pain. But if we are honest with ourselves, we have to admit that sorrow does more to refine our character and conform us to the image of Christ than pleasure and comfort do. Tough times are opportunities to draw closer to God.

Mary, who attended my classes on Living Through Loss, is an example of this truth. She and her husband were faithful workers in their church. Then the pressures of life began to tug and pull them in other directions, and church no longer seemed to be a priority. Her husband had chronic illnesses, but no one expected him to collapse and die suddenly of a heart attack. When that happened, Mary faced the greatest challenge ever to her faith.

She struggled with overwhelming grief as she returned to work as a bank teller just two weeks after her husband's death. She had trouble concentrating, remembering, and thinking logically. Her shock and grief left her in a fog of confusion. As she grappled with loneliness and despair, she kept thinking, Something is wrong. What am I missing?

Then God impressed on her confused mind the need to get back into His Word for comfort, peace and strength. She learned what those in this book have found over and over again: trials can draw us closer to God. The Bible seemed alive and powerful as she found comfort from such Scriptures as:

"The LORD is my light and my salvation—whom shall I fear? The LORD is the stronghold of my life—of whom shall I be afraid?" (Psalm 27:1)

"In you, O LORD, I have taken refuge; let me never be put to shame; deliver me in your righteousness" (Psalm 31:1).

Even though we draw closer to God, we may still have many unanswered questions. Most of the people I interviewed described their grieving time as a painful attempt to understand God's purposes in their loss. Not one of them has received an answer to the question, "Why?" In times of loss, our patience and our faith are tested and strengthened. One of the signs that our faith is growing stronger is when we are able to trust God even when our "Why?" questions go unanswered in this life. Someday, in eternity, all will be explained. But for now, we simply have to trust and cling to God, knowing that His ways—while not our ways—are nevertheless the best ways of all.

5. God is the best comforter.

"Praise be to the God and Father of our Lord Jesus Christ, the Father of compassion and the God of all comfort, who comforts us in all our troubles . . . " (2 Corinthians 1:3-4). The people who have shared their stories in this book have shown that as we read and immerse ourselves in God's Word, He speaks comfort to us. He has given us the Scriptures, not only to instruct us but to heal us. Through His Word, we experience a release from pent-up emotions as we pour out our grief to Him. "He will call upon me, and I will answer him. I will be with him in trouble. I will deliver him and honor him" (Psalm 91:15).

The people in this book have shared their difficulty in keeping a proper perspective in the midst of suffering. It is easy for our view to become distorted and self-centered because of our pain. We may come to believe that no one else has ever suffered as much as we have.

But as we meditate on God's blessings, even in our calamity, we can find something to give thanks for. Reminding ourselves of God's love and faithfulness, regardless of our feelings, is essential to healthy grieving. "How priceless is your unfailing love! Both high and low among men find refuge in the shadow of your wings" (Psalm 36:7). "Because of the Lord's great love we are not consumed, for his compassions never fail. They are new every morning; great is your faithfulness" (Lamentations 3:22-23).

In every story related here, God has given hope, courage, confidence, and strength as needed. These stories affirm the fact that no human comforter can soothe aching, broken hearts as well as God can. "He heals the brokenhearted and binds up their wounds" (Psalm 147:3). This is the truth we cling to, the hope that restores our souls, as we move beyond grief, and into His joy and His peace.

....

CONSIDER HIM

When the storm is raging high,
When the tempest rends the sky,
When my eyes with tears are dim,
Then, my soul, consider Him.

When my plans are in the dust,
When my dearest hopes are crushed,
When is passed each foolish whim,
Then, my soul, consider Him.

When with dearest friends I part,
When deep sorrow fills my heart,
When pain rocks each weary limb,
Then, my soul, consider Him.

When I track my weary way,
When fresh trials come each day.
When my faith and hope are dim,
Then, my soul, consider Him.

Clouds or sunshine, dark or bright,
Evening shades or morning light,
When my cup flows o'er the brim,
Then, my soul, consider Him.

—Author unknown

Note to the Reader

The publisher invites you to share your response to the message of this book by writing Discovery House Publishers, P. O. Box 3566, Grand Rapids, MI 49501, U.S.A. or by calling 1-800-653-8333. For information about other Discovery House publications, contact us at the same address and phone number.